The Federal Reserve System

PURPOSES & FUNCTIONS

Board of Governors of the Federal Reserve System
Washington, D.C.

First Edition, May 1939
Second Edition, November 1947
Third Edition, April 1954
Fourth Edition, February 1961
Fifth Edition, December 1963
Sixth Edition, September 1974
Seventh Edition, December 1984
Eighth Edition, December 1994
Ninth Edition, June 2005

Library of Congress Control Number 39026719

Copies of this book may be obtained from Publications
Fulfillment, Board of Governors of the Federal Reserve System,
Washington, DC 20551.

Purposes and Functions is published under the direction of the
staff Publications Committee. It is assisted by the Publications
Department, under the direction of Lucretia M. Boyer.

Preface

This is the ninth edition of The Federal Reserve System: Purposes and Functions. *It has been revised by staff members of the Federal Reserve Board to reflect the changes that have taken place in the monetary, regulatory, and other policy areas since publication of the eighth edition in 1994. It incorporates major changes in the law and in the structure of the financial system that have occurred over the past decade.*

The Board's Publications Committee had overall responsibility for the preparation of this edition. Major contributions were made by the following:

Division of Research and Statistics
Thomas D. Simpson

Division of Monetary Affairs
Cheryl L. Edwards, William R. Nelson, Seth B. Carpenter, and Selva Demiralp

Division of International Finance
Joseph E. Gagnon

Division of Banking Supervision and Regulation
Richard Spillenkothen, Virginia M. Gibbs, and Greg Feldberg

Division of Consumer and Community Affairs
Jeanne Hogarth, Adrienne Hurt, Terri Johnsen, Elizabeth Eurgubian, Yvonne Cooper, and Tracy Anderson

Division of Reserve Bank Operations and Payment Systems
Jeffrey C. Marquardt and Theresa A. Trimble

Legal Division
Kieran Fallon, Joshua H. Kaplan, Amanda Allexon, and Heatherun Allison

Office of Board Members
Rose Pianalto, Diana Lahm, Anita Bennett, and Britt Leckman

Contents

The Federal Reserve System is the central bank of the United States. It was founded by Congress in 1913 to provide the nation with a safer, more flexible, and more stable monetary and financial system. Over the years, its role in banking and the economy has expanded.

Today, the Federal Reserve's duties fall into four general areas:

- conducting the nation's monetary policy by influencing the monetary and credit conditions in the economy in pursuit of maximum employment, stable prices, and moderate long-term interest rates
- supervising and regulating banking institutions to ensure the safety and soundness of the nation's banking and financial system and to protect the credit rights of consumers
- maintaining the stability of the financial system and containing systemic risk that may arise in financial markets
- providing financial services to depository institutions, the U.S. government, and foreign official institutions, including playing a major role in operating the nation's payments system

Most developed countries have a central bank whose functions are broadly similar to those of the Federal Reserve. The oldest, Sweden's Riksbank, has existed since 1668 and the Bank of England since 1694. Napoleon I established the Banque de France in 1800, and the Bank of Canada began operations in 1935. The German Bundesbank was reestablished after World War II and is loosely modeled on the Federal Reserve. More recently, some functions of the Banque de France and the Bundesbank have been assumed by the European Central Bank, formed in 1998.

Background

During the nineteenth century and the beginning of the twentieth century, financial panics plagued the nation, leading to bank failures and business bankruptcies that severely disrupted the economy. The failure of the nation's banking system to effectively provide funding to troubled depository institutions contributed significantly to the economy's vulnerability to financial panics. Short-term credit is an important source of liquidity when a bank experiences unexpected and widespread withdrawals during a financial panic. A particularly severe crisis in 1907 prompted

Congress to establish the National Monetary Commission, which put forth proposals to create an institution that would help prevent and contain financial disruptions of this kind. After considerable debate, Congress passed the Federal Reserve Act "to provide for the establishment of Federal reserve banks, to furnish an elastic currency, to afford means of rediscounting commercial paper, to establish a more effective supervision of banking in the United States, and for other purposes." President Woodrow Wilson signed the act into law on December 23, 1913.

President Wilson signed the Federal Reserve Act on December 23, 1913.

Soon after the creation of the Federal Reserve, it became clear that the act had broader implications for national economic and financial policy. As time has passed, further legislation has clarified and supplemented the original purposes. Key laws affecting the Federal Reserve have been the Banking Act of 1935; the Employment Act of 1946; the Bank Holding Company Act of 1956 and the amendments of 1970; the International Banking Act of 1978; the Full Employment and Balanced Growth Act of 1978; the Depository Institutions Deregulation and Monetary Control Act of 1980; the Financial Institutions Reform, Recovery, and Enforcement Act of 1989; the Federal Deposit Insurance Corporation Improvement Act of 1991; and the Gramm-Leach-Bliley Act of 1999. Congress has also adopted legislation defining the primary objectives of national economic policy, including the Employment Act of 1946; the Federal Reserve Reform Act of 1977; and the Full Employment and Balanced Growth Act of 1978, which is sometimes called the Humphrey-Hawkins Act, after its original sponsors. These objectives include economic growth in line with the economy's potential to expand; a high level of employment; stable prices (that is, stability in the purchasing power of the dollar); and moderate long-term interest rates.

The Federal Reserve System is considered to be an independent central bank because its decisions do not have to be ratified by the President or anyone else in the executive branch of government. The System is, however, subject to oversight by the U.S. Congress. The Federal Reserve must work within the framework of the overall objectives of economic and financial policy established by the government; therefore, the description of the System as "independent within the government" is more accurate.

Structure of the System

Congress designed the structure of the Federal Reserve System to give it a broad perspective on the economy and on economic activity in all parts of the nation. It is a federal system, composed of a central, governmental agency—the Board of Governors—in Washington, D.C., and twelve regional Federal Reserve Banks. The Board and the Reserve Banks share responsibility for supervising and regulating certain financial institutions and activities, for providing banking services to depository institutions and the federal government, and for ensuring that consumers receive adequate information and fair treatment in their business with the banking system.

The Federal Reserve must work within the framework of the overall objectives of economic and financial policy established by the government.

A major component of the System is the Federal Open Market Committee (FOMC), which is made up of the members of the Board of Governors, the president of the Federal Reserve Bank of New York, and presidents of four other Federal Reserve Banks, who serve on a rotating basis. The FOMC oversees open market operations, which is the main tool used by the Federal Reserve to influence overall monetary and credit conditions. These operations are described in greater detail in chapter 3.

The Federal Reserve implements monetary policy through its control over the federal funds rate—the rate at which depository institutions trade balances at the Federal Reserve. It exercises this control by influencing the demand for and supply of these balances through the following means:

- Open market operations—the purchase or sale of securities, primarily U.S. Treasury securities, in the open market to influence the level of balances that depository institutions hold at the Federal Reserve Banks
- Reserve requirements—requirements regarding the percentage of certain deposits that depository institutions must hold in reserve in the form of cash or in an account at a Federal Reserve Bank
- Contractual clearing balances—an amount that a depository institution agrees to hold at its Federal Reserve Bank in addition to any required reserve balance
- Discount window lending—extensions of credit to depository institutions made through the primary, secondary, or seasonal lending programs

Two other groups play roles in the functioning of the Federal Reserve System: depository institutions, through which monetary policy operates, and advisory committees, which make recommendations to the Board of Governors and to the Reserve Banks regarding the System's responsibilities.

Board of Governors

The Board of Governors of the Federal Reserve System is a federal government agency. The Board is composed of seven members, who are appointed by the President of the United States and confirmed by the U.S. Senate. The full term of a Board member is fourteen years, and the appointments are staggered so that one term expires on January 31 of each even-numbered year. After serving a full term, a Board member may not be reappointed. If a member leaves the Board before his or her term expires, however, the person appointed and confirmed to serve the remainder of the term may later be reappointed to a full term.

The first Federal Reserve Board, 1914

The Chairman and the Vice Chairman of the Board are also appointed by the President and confirmed by the Senate. The nominees to these posts must already be members of the Board or must be simultaneously appointed to the Board. The terms for these positions are four years.

The Board of Governors is supported by a staff in Washington, D.C., numbering about 1,800 as of 2004. The Board's responsibilities require thorough analysis of domestic and international financial and economic developments. The Board carries out those responsibilities in conjunction with other components of the Federal Reserve System. The Board of Governors also supervises and regulates the operations of the Federal Reserve Banks, exercises broad responsibility in the nation's payments system, and administers most of the nation's laws regarding consumer credit protection.

Policy regarding open market operations is established by the FOMC. However, the Board of Governors has sole authority over changes in reserve requirements, and it must approve any change in the discount rate initiated by a Federal Reserve Bank.

The Board also plays a major role in the supervision and regulation of the U.S. banking system. It has supervisory responsibilities for state-chartered banks that are members of the Federal Reserve System, bank holding companies (companies that control banks), the foreign activities of member banks, the U.S. activities of foreign banks, and Edge Act and agreement corporations (limited-purpose institutions that engage in a foreign banking business). The Board and, under delegated authority, the Federal

Reserve Banks, supervise approximately 900 state member banks and 5,000 bank holding companies. Other federal agencies also serve as the primary federal supervisors of commercial banks; the Office of the Comptroller of the Currency supervises national banks, and the Federal Deposit Insurance Corporation supervises state banks that are not members of the Federal Reserve System.

Some regulations issued by the Board apply to the entire banking industry, whereas others apply only to member banks, that is, state banks that have chosen to join the Federal Reserve System and national banks, which by law must be members of the System. The Board also issues regulations to carry out major federal laws governing consumer credit protection, such as the Truth in Lending, Equal Credit Opportunity, and Home Mortgage Disclosure Acts. Many of these consumer protection regulations apply to various lenders outside the banking industry as well as to banks.

Members of the Board of Governors are in continual contact with other policy makers in government. They frequently testify before congressional committees on the economy, monetary policy, banking supervision and regulation, consumer credit protection, financial markets, and other matters. For instance, as required by the Federal Reserve Act, the Chairman of the Board of Governors testifies before the Senate Committee on Banking, Housing, and Urban Affairs and the House Committee on Financial Services on or about February 20 and July 20 of each year. The Chairman's testimony addresses the efforts, activities, objectives, and plans of the Board of Governors and the Federal Open Market Committee with respect to the conduct of monetary policy, as well as economic developments in the United States and the prospects for the future. Concurrently, the Board of Governors must submit a report on these same issues to the House and Senate committees before which the Chairman testifies.

The Board has regular contact with members of the President's Council of Economic Advisers and other key economic officials. The Chairman also meets from time to time with the President of the United States and has regular meetings with the Secretary of the Treasury.

The Chairman has formal responsibilities in the international arena as well. For example, he is the alternate U.S. member of the board of governors of the International Monetary Fund, a member of the board of the Bank for International Settlements (BIS), and a member, along with the heads of other relevant U.S. agencies and departments, of the National Advisory Council on International Monetary and Financial Policies. He is also a member of U.S. delegations to key international meetings, such as those of the finance ministers and central bank governors of the seven largest industrial countries—referred to as the Group of Seven, or G-7. He, other Board members, and Board staff members share many international responsibilities, including representing the Federal Reserve at meetings at the BIS in Basel, Switzerland, and at the Organisation for Economic Co-operation and Development in Paris, France.

One member of the Board of Governors serves as the System's representative to the Federal Financial Institutions Examination Council (FFIEC), which is responsible for coordinating, at the federal level, examinations of depository institutions and related policies. The FFIEC has representatives from the Federal Deposit Insurance Corporation, the National Credit Union Administration, the Office of the Comptroller of the Currency, and the Office of Thrift Supervision, as well.

The Board publishes detailed statistics and other information about the System's activities and the economy in publications such as the quarterly *Federal Reserve Bulletin*, the monthly *Statistical Supplement*, and separate statistical releases. Through the *Federal Reserve Regulatory Service*, it provides materials relating to its regulatory and supervisory functions. Extensive information about the Board of Governors is available on the Board's web site (www.federalreserve.gov), including the testimony and speeches of Board members; actions on banking and consumer regulations and other matters; and statistics and research papers concerning economic, banking, and financial matters.

The Reserve Banks are the operating arms of the central banking system.

The Board is audited annually by a major public accounting firm. In addition, the Government Accountability Office (GAO) generally exercises its authority to conduct a number of reviews each year to look at specific aspects of the Federal Reserve's activities. The audit report of the public accounting firm and a complete list of GAO reviews under way are available in the Board's *Annual Report*, which is sent to Congress during the second quarter of each calendar year. Monetary policy is exempt from audit by the GAO because it is monitored directly by Congress through written reports, including the semiannual *Monetary Policy Report to the Congress*, prepared by the Board of Governors.

Federal Reserve Banks

A network of twelve Federal Reserve Banks and their Branches (twenty-five as of 2004) carries out a variety of System functions, including operating a nationwide payments system, distributing the nation's currency and coin, supervising and regulating member banks and bank holding companies, and serving as banker for the U.S. Treasury. The twelve Reserve Banks are each responsible for a particular geographic area or district of the United States. Each Reserve District is identified by a number and a letter (see the list of District offices on page 7). Besides carrying out functions for the System as a whole, such as administering nationwide banking and credit policies, each Reserve Bank acts as a depository for the banks in its own District and fulfills other District responsibilities. The various

Federal Reserve District Banks and Branches

Number	Letter	Bank	Branch
1	A	Boston	
2	B	New York	Buffalo, New York
3	C	Philadelphia	
4	D	Cleveland	Cincinnati, Ohio Pittsburgh, Pennsylvania
5	E	Richmond	Baltimore, Maryland Charlotte, North Carolina
6	F	Atlanta	Birmingham, Alabama Jacksonville, Florida Miami, Florida Nashville, Tennessee New Orleans, Louisiana
7	G	Chicago	Detroit, Michigan
8	H	St. Louis	Little Rock, Arkansas Louisville, Kentucky Memphis, Tennessee
9	I	Minneapolis	Helena, Montana
10	J	Kansas City	Denver, Colorado Oklahoma City, Oklahoma Omaha, Nebraska
11	K	Dallas	El Paso, Texas Houston, Texas San Antonio, Texas
12	L	San Francisco	Los Angeles, California Portland, Oregon Salt Lake City, Utah Seattle, Washington

The Federal Reserve System

Legend

- ■ Federal Reserve Bank city
- ★ Board of Governors of the Federal Reserve System, Washington, D.C.
- • Federal Reserve Branch city
- — Branch boundary

Notes

The Federal Reserve officially identifies Districts by number and by Reserve Bank city (shown on both pages) as well as by letter (shown on the facing page).

In the 12th District, the Seattle Branch serves Alaska and the San Francisco Bank serves Hawaii.

The New York Bank serves the Commonwealth of Puerto Rico and the U.S. Virgin Islands; the San Francisco Bank serves American Samoa, Guam, and the Commonwealth of the Northern Mariana Islands.

The Board of Governors revised the Branch boundaries of the System most recently in February 1996.

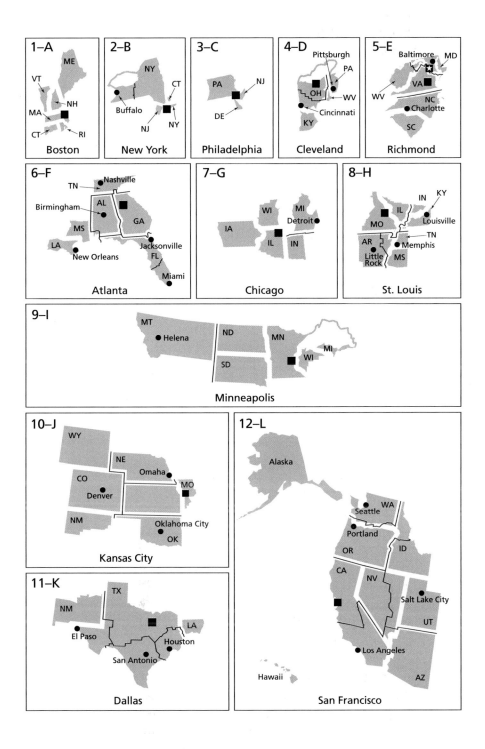

offices and boundaries of the Federal Reserve Districts are shown on the maps on pages 8 and 9.

The Board of Governors has broad oversight responsibility for the operations and activities of the Federal Reserve Banks and their Branches. This authority includes oversight of the Reserve Banks' services to banks and other depository institutions and of their examination and supervision of various banking institutions. Each Federal Reserve Bank must submit its annual budget to the Board of Governors for approval. Particular types of expenditures—such as those for construction or major alterations of Reserve Bank buildings and for the salaries of Reserve Bank presidents and first vice presidents—also are subject to specific Board approval.

Congress chartered the Federal Reserve Banks for a public purpose. The Reserve Banks are the operating arms of the central banking system, and they combine both public and private elements in their makeup and organization. As part of the Federal Reserve System, the Banks are subject to oversight by Congress.

Each Reserve Bank has its own board of nine directors chosen from outside the Bank as provided by law. The boards of the Reserve Banks are intended to represent a cross-section of banking, commercial, agricultural, industrial, and public interests within the Federal Reserve District. Three directors, designated Class A directors, represent commercial banks that are members of the Federal Reserve System. Three Class B and three Class C directors represent the public. The member commercial banks in each District elect the Class A and Class B directors. The Board of Governors appoints the Class C directors to their posts. From the Class C directors, the Board of Governors selects one person as chairman and another as deputy chairman. No Class B or Class C director may be an officer, director, or employee of a bank or a bank holding company. No Class C director may own stock in a bank or a bank holding company. The directors in turn nominate a president and first vice president of the Reserve Bank, whose selection is subject to approval by the Board of Governors. Each Branch of a Reserve Bank has its own board of directors composed of at least three and no more than seven members. A majority of these directors are appointed by the Branch's Reserve Bank; the others are appointed by the Board of Governors.

Boards of directors of the Reserve Banks provide the Federal Reserve System with a wealth of information on economic conditions in virtually every corner of the nation. This information is used by the FOMC and the Board of Governors in reaching major decisions about monetary policy. Information from directors and other sources gathered by the Reserve Banks is also shared with the public in a special report—informally called the Beige Book—which is issued about two weeks before each meeting of the FOMC. In addition, every two weeks, the board of each Bank must recommend interest rates for its Bank's discount window lending, subject to review and determination by the Board of Governors.

The income of the Federal Reserve System is derived primarily from the interest on U.S. government securities that it has acquired through open market operations. Other major sources of income are the interest on foreign currency investments held by the System; interest on loans to depository institutions; and fees received for services provided to depository institutions, such as check clearing, funds transfers, and automated clearinghouse operations.

After it pays its expenses, the Federal Reserve turns the rest of its earnings over to the U.S. Treasury. About 95 percent of the Reserve Banks' net earnings have been paid into the Treasury since the Federal Reserve System began operations in 1914. (Income and expenses of the Federal Reserve Banks from 1914 to the present are included in the *Annual Report* of the Board of Governors.) In 2003, the Federal Reserve paid approximately $22 billion to the Treasury.

After it pays its expenses, the Federal Reserve turns the rest of its earnings over to the U.S. Treasury.

The Board of Governors contracts with an accounting firm to conduct an audit of the Reserve Banks every year, and Board staff periodically reviews the operations of the Reserve Banks in key functional areas. The audited combined financial statements of the Reserve Banks are published in the Board's *Annual Report*. The Reserve Banks, like the Board, are subject to audit by the GAO, but certain functions, such as transactions with foreign central banks and open market operations, are excluded from the GAO's audit. Each Reserve Bank has an internal auditor who is responsible to the Bank's board of directors.

Federal Open Market Committee

The FOMC is charged under law with overseeing open market operations, the principal tool of national monetary policy. These operations affect the amount of Federal Reserve balances available to depository institutions (see chapter 3), thereby influencing overall monetary and credit conditions. The FOMC also directs operations undertaken by the Federal Reserve in foreign exchange markets.

The FOMC is composed of the seven members of the Board of Governors and five of the twelve Reserve Bank presidents. The president of the Federal Reserve Bank of New York is a permanent member; the other presidents serve one-year terms on a rotating basis.[1] All the presidents participate in FOMC discussions, contributing to the committee's assessment of the economy and of policy options, but only the five presidents who are committee members vote on policy decisions. The FOMC, under law, determines its own internal organization and by tradition elects the Chairman of the Board of Governors as its chairman and the president of the Federal Reserve Bank of New York as its vice chairman. Formal meetings typically are held eight times each year in Washington, D.C. Telephone consultations and other meetings are held when needed.

Member Banks

The FOMC is composed of the seven members of the Board of Governors and five of the twelve Reserve Bank presidents.

The nation's commercial banks can be divided into three types according to which governmental body charters them and whether or not they are members of the Federal Reserve System. Those chartered by the federal government (through the Office of the Comptroller of the Currency in the Department of the Treasury) are national banks; by law, they are members of the Federal Reserve System. Banks chartered by the states are divided into those that are members of the Federal Reserve System (state member banks) and those that are not (state nonmember banks). State banks are not required to join the Federal Reserve System, but they may elect to become members if they meet the standards set by the Board of Governors. As of March 2004, of the nation's approximately 7,700 commercial banks approximately 2,900 were members of the Federal Reserve System—approximately 2,000 national banks and 900 state banks.

Member banks must subscribe to stock in their regional Federal Reserve Bank in an amount equal to 6 percent of their capital and surplus, half of which must be paid in while the other half is subject to call by the Board of Governors. The holding of this stock, however, does not carry with it the control and financial interest conveyed to holders of common stock in for-profit organizations. It is merely a legal obligation of Federal Reserve membership, and the stock may not be sold or pledged as collateral for loans. Member banks receive a 6 percent dividend annually on their stock, as specified by law, and vote for the Class A and Class B directors of the Reserve Bank. Stock in Federal Reserve Banks is not available for purchase by individuals or entities other than member banks.

---

1. The rotating seats are filled from the following four groups of Banks, one Bank president from each group: Boston, Philadelphia, and Richmond; Cleveland and Chicago; Atlanta, St. Louis, and Dallas; and Minneapolis, Kansas City, and San Francisco. An alternate for each Reserve Bank president also is elected. This alternate, who must be a president or first vice president of a Reserve Bank, may serve on the FOMC in the absence of the relevant Reserve Bank president.

Advisory Committees

The Federal Reserve System uses advisory committees in carrying out its varied responsibilities. Three of these committees advise the Board of Governors directly:

- *Federal Advisory Council.* This council, which is composed of twelve representatives of the banking industry, consults with and advises the Board on all matters within the Board's jurisdiction. It ordinarily meets four times a year, as required by the Federal Reserve Act. These meetings are held in Washington, D.C., customarily on the first Friday of February, May, September, and December, although occasionally the meetings are set for different times to suit the convenience of either the council or the Board. Annually, each Reserve Bank chooses one person to represent its District on the Federal Advisory Committee, and members customarily serve three one-year terms and elect their own officers.
- *Consumer Advisory Council.* This council, established in 1976, advises the Board on the exercise of its responsibilities under the Consumer Credit Protection Act and on other matters in the area of consumer financial services. The council's membership represents the interests of consumers, communities, and the financial services industry. Members are appointed by the Board of Governors and serve staggered three-year terms. The council meets three times a year in Washington, D.C., and the meetings are open to the public.
- *Thrift Institutions Advisory Council.* After the passage of the Depository Institutions Deregulation and Monetary Control Act of 1980, which extended to thrift institutions the Federal Reserve's reserve requirements and access to the discount window, the Board of Governors established this council to obtain information and views on the special needs and problems of thrift institutions. Unlike the Federal Advisory Council and the Consumer Advisory Council, the Thrift Institutions Advisory Council is not a statutorily mandated body, but it performs a comparable function in providing firsthand advice from representatives of institutions that have an important relationship with the Federal Reserve. The council meets with the Board in Washington, D.C., three times a year. The members are representatives from savings and loan institutions, mutual savings banks, and credit unions. Members are appointed by the Board of Governors and generally serve for two years.

The Federal Reserve Banks also use advisory committees. Of these advisory committees, perhaps the most important are the committees (one for each Reserve Bank) that advise the Banks on matters of agriculture, small business, and labor. Biannually, the Board solicits the views of each of these committees by mail.

The Federal Reserve sets the nation's monetary policy to promote the objectives of maximum employment, stable prices, and moderate long-term interest rates. The challenge for policy makers is that tensions among the goals can arise in the short run and that information about the economy becomes available only with a lag and may be imperfect.

Goals of Monetary Policy

The goals of monetary policy are spelled out in the Federal Reserve Act, which specifies that the Board of Governors and the Federal Open Market Committee should seek "to promote effectively the goals of maximum employment, stable prices, and moderate long-term interest rates." Stable prices in the long run are a precondition for maximum sustainable output growth and employment as well as moderate long-term interest rates. When prices are stable and believed likely to remain so, the prices of goods, services, materials, and labor are undistorted by inflation and serve as clearer signals and guides to the efficient allocation of resources and thus contribute to higher standards of living. Moreover, stable prices foster saving and capital formation, because when the risk of erosion of asset values resulting from inflation—and the need to guard against such losses—are minimized, households are encouraged to save more and businesses are encouraged to invest more.

Although price stability can help achieve maximum sustainable output growth and employment over the longer run, in the short run some tension can exist between the two goals. Often, a slowing of employment is accompanied by lessened pressures on prices, and moving to counter the weakening of the labor market by easing policy does not have adverse inflationary effects. Sometimes, however, upward pressures on prices are developing as output and employment are softening—especially when an adverse supply shock, such as a spike in energy prices, has occurred. Then, an attempt to restrain inflation pressures would compound the weakness in the economy, or an attempt to reverse employment losses would aggravate inflation. In such circumstances, those responsible for monetary policy face a dilemma and must decide whether to focus on defusing price pressures or on cushioning the loss of employment and output. Adding to the difficulty is the possibility that an expectation of increasing inflation might get built into decisions about prices and wages, thereby adding to inflation inertia and making it more difficult to achieve price stability.

Beyond influencing the level of prices and the level of output in the near term, the Federal Reserve can contribute to financial stability and better economic performance by acting to contain financial disruptions and preventing their spread outside the financial sector. Modern financial systems are highly complex and interdependent and may be vulnerable to wide-scale systemic disruptions, such as those that can occur during a plunge in stock prices. The Federal Reserve can enhance the financial system's resilience to such shocks through its regulatory policies toward banking institutions and payment systems. If a threatening disturbance develops, the Federal Reserve can also cushion the impact on financial markets and the economy by aggressively and visibly providing liquidity through open market operations or discount window lending.

How Monetary Policy Affects the Economy

The initial link in the chain between monetary policy and the economy is the market for balances held at the Federal Reserve Banks. Depository institutions have accounts at their Reserve Banks, and they actively trade balances held in these accounts in the federal funds market at an interest rate known as the federal funds rate. The Federal Reserve exercises considerable control over the federal funds rate through its influence over the supply of and demand for balances at the Reserve Banks.

The FOMC sets the federal funds rate at a level it believes will foster financial and monetary conditions consistent with achieving its monetary policy objectives, and it adjusts that target in line with evolving economic developments. A change in the federal funds rate, or even a change in expectations about the future level of the federal funds rate, can set off a chain of events that will affect other short-term interest rates, longer-term interest rates, the foreign exchange value of the dollar, and stock prices. In turn, changes in these variables will affect households' and businesses' spending decisions, thereby affecting growth in aggregate demand and the economy.

Short-term interest rates, such as those on Treasury bills and commercial paper, are affected not only by the current level of the federal funds rate but also by expectations about the overnight federal funds rate over the duration of the short-term contract. As a result, short-term interest rates could decline if the Federal Reserve surprised market participants with a reduction in the federal funds rate, or if unfolding events convinced participants that the Federal Reserve was going to be holding the federal funds rate lower than had been anticipated. Similarly, short-term inter-

Depository institutions have accounts at their Reserve Banks, and they actively trade balances held in these accounts in the federal funds market at an interest rate known as the federal funds rate.

est rates would increase if the Federal Reserve surprised market participants by announcing an increase in the federal funds rate, or if some event prompted market participants to believe that the Federal Reserve was going to be holding the federal funds rate at higher levels than had been anticipated.

It is for these reasons that market participants closely follow data releases and statements by Federal Reserve officials, watching for clues that the economy and prices are on a different trajectory than had been thought, which would have implications for the stance of monetary policy.

Changes in short-term interest rates will influence long-term interest rates, such as those on Treasury notes, corporate bonds, fixed-rate mortgages, and auto and other consumer loans. Long-term rates are affected not only by changes in current short-term rates but also by expectations about short-term rates over the rest of the life of the long-term contract. Generally, economic news or statements by officials will have a greater impact on short-term interest rates than on longer rates because they typically have a bearing on the course of the economy and monetary policy over a shorter period; however, the impact on long rates can also be considerable because the news has clear implications for the expected course of short-term rates over a long period.

Lower interest rates in the United States will lead to a decline in the exchange value of the dollar, prompting an increase in the price of imports and a decline in the price of exports.

Changes in long-term interest rates also affect stock prices, which can have a pronounced effect on household wealth. Investors try to keep their investment returns on stocks in line with the return on bonds, after allowing for the greater riskiness of stocks. For example, if long-term interest rates decline, then, all else being equal, returns on stocks will exceed returns on bonds and encourage investors to purchase stocks and bid up stock prices to the point at which expected risk-adjusted returns on stocks are once again aligned with returns on bonds. Moreover, lower interest rates may convince investors that the economy will be stronger and profits higher in the near future, which should further lift equity prices.

Furthermore, changes in monetary policy affect the exchange value of the dollar on currency markets. For example, if interest rates rise in the United States, yields on dollar assets will look more favorable, which will lead to bidding up of the dollar on foreign exchange markets. The higher dollar will lower the cost of imports to U.S. residents and raise the price of U.S. exports to those living outside the United States. Conversely, lower interest rates in the United States will lead to a decline in the exchange value of the dollar, prompting an increase in the price of imports and a decline in the price of exports.

Changes in the value of financial assets, whether the result of an actual or expected change in monetary policy, will affect a wide range of spending decisions. For example, a drop in interest rates, a lower exchange value of the dollar, and higher stock prices will stimulate various types of spending. Investment projects that businesses believed would be only marginally profitable will become more attractive with lower financing costs. Lower consumer loan rates will elicit greater demand for consumer goods, especially bigger-ticket items such as motor vehicles. Lower mortgage rates will make housing more affordable and lead to more home purchases. They will also encourage mortgage refinancing, which will reduce ongoing housing costs and enable households to purchase other goods. When refinancing, some homeowners may withdraw a portion of their home equity to pay for other things, such as a motor vehicle, other consumer goods, or a long-desired vacation trip. Higher stock prices can also add to household wealth and to the ability to make purchases that had previously seemed beyond reach. The reduction in the value of the dollar associated with a drop in interest rates will tend to boost U.S. exports by lowering the cost of U.S. goods and services in foreign markets. It will also make imported goods more expensive, which will encourage businesses and households to purchase domestically produced goods instead. All of these responses will strengthen growth in aggregate demand. A tightening of monetary policy will have the opposite effect on spending and will moderate growth of aggregate demand.

If the economy slows and employment softens, policy makers will be inclined to ease monetary policy to stimulate aggregate demand.

If the economy slows and employment softens, policy makers will be inclined to ease monetary policy to stimulate aggregate demand. When growth in aggregate demand is boosted above growth in the economy's potential to produce, slack in the economy will be absorbed and employment will return to a more sustainable path. In contrast, if the economy is showing signs of overheating and inflation pressures are building, the Federal Reserve will be inclined to counter these pressures by tightening monetary policy—to bring growth in aggregate demand below that of the economy's potential to produce—for as long as necessary to defuse the inflationary pressures and put the economy on a path to sustainable expansion.

While these policy choices seem reasonably straightforward, monetary policy makers routinely face certain notable uncertainties. First, the actual position of the economy and growth in aggregate demand at any point in time are only partially known, as key information on spending, production, and prices becomes available only with a lag. Therefore, policy makers must rely on estimates of these economic variables when assessing the appropriate course of policy, aware that they could act on the basis of misleading information. Second, exactly how a given adjustment in the federal funds rate will affect growth in aggregate demand—in terms of both the overall magnitude and the timing of its impact—is never certain. Economic models can provide rules of thumb for how the economy will respond, but these rules of thumb are subject to statistical error. Third, the growth in aggregate supply, often called the growth in potential output, cannot be measured with certainty. Key here is the growth of the labor force and associated labor input, as well as underlying growth in labor productivity. Growth in labor input typically can be measured with more accuracy than underlying productivity; for some time, growth in labor input has tended to be around the growth in the overall population of 1 percentage point per year. However, underlying productivity growth has varied considerably over recent decades, from approximately 1 percent or so per year to somewhere in the neighborhood of 3 percent or even higher, getting a major boost during the mid- and late 1990s from applications of information technology and advanced management systems. If, for example, productivity growth is 2 percent per year, then growth in aggregate supply would be the sum of this amount and labor input growth of 1 percent—that is, 3 percent per year. In which case, growth in aggregate demand in excess of 3 percent per year would result in a pickup in growth in employment in excess of that of the labor force and a reduction in unemployment. In contrast, growth in aggregate demand below 3 percent would result in a softening of the labor market and, in time, a reduction in inflationary pressures.

Limitations of Monetary Policy

Monetary policy is not the only force acting on output, employment, and prices. Many other factors affect aggregate demand and aggregate supply and, consequently, the economic position of households and businesses. Some of these factors can be anticipated and built into spending and other economic decisions, and some come as a surprise. On the demand side, the government influences the economy through changes in taxes and spending programs, which typically receive a lot of public attention and are therefore anticipated. For example, the effect of a tax cut may precede its actual implementation as businesses and households alter their spending in anticipation of the lower taxes. Also, forward-looking financial markets may build such fiscal events into the level and structure of interest rates, so that a stimulative measure, such as a tax cut, would tend to raise the level of interest rates even before the tax cut becomes effective, which will have a restraining effect on demand and the economy before the fiscal stimulus is actually applied.

Other changes in aggregate demand and supply can be totally unpredictable and influence the economy in unforeseen ways. Examples of such shocks on the demand side are shifts in consumer and business confidence, and changes in the lending posture of commercial banks and other creditors. Lessened confidence regarding the outlook for the economy and labor market or more restrictive lending conditions tend to curb business and household spending. On the supply side, natural disasters, disruptions in the oil market that reduce supply, agricultural losses, and slowdowns in

If the economy is showing signs of overheating and inflation pressures are building, the Federal Reserve will be inclined to counter these pressures by tightening monetary policy.

productivity growth are examples of adverse supply shocks. Such shocks tend to raise prices and reduce output. Monetary policy can attempt to counter the loss of output or the higher prices but cannot fully offset both.

In practice, as previously noted, monetary policy makers do not have up-to-the-minute information on the state of the economy and prices. Useful information is limited not only by lags in the construction and availability of key data but also by later revisions, which can alter the picture considerably. Therefore, although monetary policy makers will eventually be able to offset the effects that adverse demand shocks have on the economy, it will be some time before the shock is fully recognized and—given the lag between a policy action and the effect of the action on aggregate demand—an even longer time before it is countered. Add to this the uncertainty about how the economy will respond to an easing or tightening of policy of a given magnitude, and it is not hard to see how the economy and prices can depart from a desired path for a period of time.

The statutory goals of maximum employment and stable prices are easier to achieve if the public understands those goals and believes that the Federal Reserve will take effective measures to achieve them. For example, if the Federal Reserve responds to a negative demand shock to the economy with an aggressive and transparent easing of policy, businesses and consumers may believe that these actions will restore the economy to full employment; consequently, they may be less inclined to pull back on spending because of concern that demand may not be strong enough to warrant new business investment or that their job prospects may not warrant the purchase of big-ticket household goods. Similarly, a credible anti-inflation policy will lead businesses and households to expect less wage and price inflation; workers then will not feel the same need to protect themselves by demanding large wage increases, and businesses will be less aggressive in raising their prices, for fear of losing sales and profits. As a result, inflation will come down more rapidly, in keeping with the policy-related slowing in growth of aggregate demand, and will give rise to less slack in product and resource markets than if workers and businesses continued to act as if inflation were not going to slow.

The statutory goals of maximum employment and stable prices are easier to achieve if the public understands those goals and believes that the Federal Reserve will take effective measures to achieve them.

Guides to Monetary Policy

Although the goals of monetary policy are clearly spelled out in law, the means to achieve those goals are not. Changes in the FOMC's target federal funds rate take some time to affect the economy and prices, and it is often far from obvious whether a selected level of the federal funds rate will achieve those goals. For this reason, some have suggested that the Federal Reserve pay close attention to guides that are intermediate between its operational target—the federal funds rate—and the economy.

Among those frequently mentioned are monetary aggregates, the level and structure of interest rates, the so-called Taylor rule (discussed on page 23), and foreign exchange rates. Some suggest that one of these guides be selected as an intermediate target—that is, that a specific formal objective be set for the intermediate target and pursued aggressively with the policy instruments. Others suggest that these guides be used more as indictors, to be monitored regularly; in other words, the Federal Reserve could establish a reference path for the intermediate variable that it thought to be consistent with achieving the final goals of monetary policy, and actual outcomes departing appreciably from that path would be seen as suggesting that the economy might be drifting off course and that a policy adjustment might be necessary.

Monetary Aggregates

Monetary aggregates have at times been advocated as guides to monetary policy on the grounds that they may have a fairly stable relationship with the economy and can be controlled to a reasonable extent by the central bank, either through control over the supply of balances at the Federal Reserve or the federal funds rate. An increase in the federal funds rate (and other short-term interest rates), for example, will reduce the attractiveness of holding money balances relative to now higher-yielding money market instruments and thereby reduce the amount of money demanded and slow growth of the money stock. There are a few measures of the money stock—ranging from the transactions-dominated M1 to the broader M2 and M3 measures, which include other liquid balances—and these aggregates have different behaviors. (See page 22 for a description of the composition of the monetary aggregates.)

Ordinarily, the rate of money growth sought over time would be equal to the rate of nominal GDP growth implied by the objective for inflation and the objective for growth in real GDP. For example, if the objective for inflation is 1 percent in a given year and the rate of growth in real GDP associated with achieving maximum employment is 3 percent, then the guideline for growth in the money stock would be 4 percent. However, the relation between the growth in money and the growth in nominal GDP, known as "velocity," can vary, often unpredictably, and this uncertainty can add to difficulties in using monetary aggregates as a guide to policy. Indeed, in the United States and many other countries with advanced financial systems over recent decades, considerable slippage and greater complexity in the relationship between money and GDP have made it more difficult to use monetary aggregates as guides to policy. In addition, the narrow and broader aggregates often give very different signals about the need to adjust policy. Accordingly, monetary aggregates have taken on less importance in policy making over time.

The Components of the Monetary Aggregates

The Federal Reserve publishes data on three monetary aggregates. The first, M1, is made up of types of money commonly used for payment, basically currency and checking deposits. The second, M2, includes M1 plus balances that generally are similar to transaction accounts and that, for the most part, can be converted fairly readily to M1 with little or no loss of principal. The M2 measure is thought to be held primarily by households. The third aggregate, M3, includes M2 plus certain accounts that are held by entities other than individuals and are issued by banks and thrift institutions to augment M2-type balances in meeting credit demands; it also includes balances in money market mutual funds held by institutional investors.

The aggregates have had different roles in monetary policy as their reliability as guides has changed. The following details their principal components:

M1   Currency (and traveler's checks)
Demand deposits
NOW and similar interest-earning checking accounts

M2   M1
Savings deposits and money market deposit accounts
Small time deposits[1]
Retail money market mutual fund balances[2]

M3   M2
Large time deposits
Institutional money market mutual fund balances
Repurchase agreements
Eurodollars

---

1. Time deposits in amounts of less than $100,000, excluding balances in IRA and Keogh accounts at depository institutions.
2. Excludes balances held in IRA and Keogh accounts with money market mutual funds.

Interest Rates

Interest rates have frequently been proposed as a guide to policy, not only because of the role they play in a wide variety of spending decisions but also because information on interest rates is available on a real-time basis. Arguing against giving interest rates the primary role in guiding monetary policy is uncertainty about exactly what level or path of interest rates is consistent with the basic goals of monetary policy. The appropriate level of interest rates will vary with the stance of fiscal policy, changes in the pattern of household and business spending, productivity growth, and economic developments abroad. It can be difficult not only to gauge the strength of these forces but also to translate them into a path for interest rates.

The slope of the yield curve (that is, the difference between the interest rate on longer-term and shorter-term instruments) has also been suggested as a guide to monetary policy. Whereas short-term interest rates are strongly influenced by the current setting of the policy instrument, longer-term interest rates are influenced by expectations of future short-term interest rates and thus by the longer-term effects of monetary policy on inflation and output. For example, a yield curve with a steeply positive slope (that is, longer-term interest rates far above short-term rates) may be a signal that participants in the bond market believe that monetary policy has become too expansive and thus, without a monetary policy correction, more inflationary. Conversely, a yield curve with a downward slope (short-term rates above longer rates) may be an indication that policy is too restrictive, perhaps risking an unwanted loss of output and employment. However, the yield curve is also influenced by other factors, including prospective fiscal policy, developments in foreign exchange markets, and expectations about the future path of monetary policy. Thus, signals from the yield curve must be interpreted carefully.

The Taylor Rule

The "Taylor rule," named after the prominent economist John Taylor, is another guide to assessing the proper stance of monetary policy. It relates the setting of the federal funds rate to the primary objectives of monetary policy—that is, the extent to which inflation may be departing from something approximating price stability and the extent to which output and employment may be departing from their maximum sustainable levels. For example, one version of the rule calls for the federal funds rate to be set equal to the rate thought to be consistent in the long run with the achievement of full employment and price stability plus a component based on the gap between current inflation and the inflation objective less a component based on the shortfall of actual output from the full-employment level. If inflation is picking up, the Taylor rule prescribes the amount by which the federal funds rate would need to be raised or, if output and employment are weakening, the amount by which it would need to be lowered. The specific parameters of the formula are set to describe actual monetary policy behavior over a period when policy is thought to have been fairly successful in achieving its basic goals.

Although this guide has appeal, it too has shortcomings. The level of short-term interest rates associated with achieving longer-term goals, a key element in the formula, can vary over time in unpredictable ways. Moreover, the current rate of inflation and position of the economy in relation to full employment are not known because of data lags and difficulties in estimating the full-employment level of output, adding another layer of uncertainty about the appropriate setting of policy.

Foreign Exchange Rates

Exchange rate movements are an important channel through which monetary policy affects the economy, and exchange rates tend to respond promptly to a change in the federal funds rate. Moreover, information on exchange rates, like information on interest rates, is available continuously throughout the day.

Interpreting the meaning of movements in exchange rates, however, can be difficult. A decline in the foreign exchange value of the dollar, for example, could indicate that monetary policy has become, or is expected to become, more accommodative, resulting in inflation risks. But exchange rates respond to other influences as well, notably developments abroad; so a weaker dollar on foreign exchange markets could instead reflect higher interest rates abroad, which make other currencies more attractive and have fewer implications for the stance of U.S. monetary policy and the performance of the U.S. economy. Conversely, a strengthening of the dollar on foreign exchange markets could reflect a move to a more restrictive monetary policy in the United States—or expectations of such a move. But it also could reflect expectations of a lower path for interest rates elsewhere or a heightened perception of risk in foreign financial assets relative to U.S. assets.

Some have advocated taking the exchange rate guide a step further and using monetary policy to stabilize the dollar's value in terms of a particular currency or in terms of a basket of currencies. However, there is a great deal of uncertainty about which level of the exchange rate is most consistent with the basic goals of monetary policy, and selecting the wrong rate could lead to a protracted period of deflation and economic slack or to an overheated economy. Also, attempting to stabilize the exchange rate in the face of a disturbance from abroad would short-circuit the cushioning effect that the associated movement in the exchange rate would have on the U.S. economy.

Conclusion

All of the guides to monetary policy discussed here have something to do with the transmission of monetary policy to the economy. All have certain advantages; however, none has shown so consistently close a relationship with the ultimate goals of monetary policy that it can be relied on alone. Consequently, monetary policy makers have tended to use a broad range of indicators—those mentioned above along with many others, including the actual behavior of output and prices—to judge trends in the economy and to assess the stance of monetary policy.

Such an eclectic approach enables the Federal Reserve and other central banks to use all the available information in conducting monetary policy. This tack may be especially important as market structures and economic processes change in ways that reduce the utility of any single indictor. However, a downside to such an approach is the difficulty it poses in communicating the central bank's intentions to the public; the lack of a relatively simple set of procedures may make it difficult for the public to understand the actions of the Federal Reserve and to judge whether those actions are consistent with achieving its statutory goals. This downside risk can be mitigated if the central bank develops a track record of achieving favorable policy outcomes when no single guide to policy has proven reliable.

The Federal Reserve exercises considerable control over the demand for and supply of balances that depository institutions hold at the Reserve Banks. In so doing, it influences the federal funds rate and, ultimately, employment, output, and prices.

The Federal Reserve implements U.S. monetary policy by affecting conditions in the market for balances that depository institutions hold at the Federal Reserve Banks. The operating objectives or targets that it has used to effect desired conditions in this market have varied over the years. At one time, the FOMC sought to achieve a specific quantity of balances, but now it sets a target for the interest rate at which those balances are traded between depository institutions—the federal funds rate. (See "Operational Approaches over the Years" on page 28.) By conducting open market operations, imposing reserve requirements, permitting depository institutions to hold contractual clearing balances, and extending credit through its discount window facility, the Federal Reserve exercises considerable control over the demand for and supply of Federal Reserve balances and the federal funds rate. Through its control of the federal funds rate, the Federal Reserve is able to foster financial and monetary conditions consistent with its monetary policy objectives.

The Market for Federal Reserve Balances

The Federal Reserve influences the economy through the market for balances that depository institutions maintain in their accounts at Federal Reserve Banks. Depository institutions make and receive payments on behalf of their customers or themselves in these accounts. The end-of-day balances in these accounts are used to meet reserve and other balance requirements. If a depository institution anticipates that it will end the day with a larger balance than it needs, it can reduce that balance in several ways, depending on how long it expects the surplus to persist. For example, if it expects the surplus to be temporary, the institution can lend excess balances in financing markets, such as the market for repurchase agreements or the market for federal funds.

Operational Approaches over the Years

The Federal Reserve can try to achieve a desired quantity of balances at the Federal Reserve Banks or a desired price of those balances (the federal funds rate), but it may not be able to achieve both at once. The greater the emphasis on a quantity objective, the more short-run changes in the demand for balances will influence the federal funds rate. Conversely, the greater the emphasis on a funds-rate objective, the more shifts in demand will influence the quantity of balances at the Federal Reserve. Over the years, the Federal Reserve has used variations of both of these operational approaches.

During most of the 1970s, the Federal Reserve targeted the price of Federal Reserve balances. The FOMC would choose a target federal funds rate that it thought would be consistent with its objective for M1 growth over short intervals of time. The funds-rate target would be raised or lowered if M1 growth significantly exceeded or fell short of the desired rate. At times, large rate movements were needed to bring money growth back in line with the target, but the extent of the necessary policy adjustment was not always gauged accurately. Moreover, there appears to have been some reluctance to permit substantial variation in the funds rate. As a result, the FOMC did not have great success in combating the increase in inflationary pressures that resulted from oil-price shocks and excessive money growth over the decade.

By late 1979, the FOMC recognized that a change in tactics was necessary. In October, the Federal Reserve began to target the quantity of reserves—the sum of balances at the Federal Reserve and cash in the vaults of depository institutions that is used to meet reserve requirements—to achieve greater control over M1 and bring down inflation. In particular, the operational objective for open market operations was a specific level of nonborrowed reserves, or total reserves less the quantity of discount window borrowing. A predetermined target path for nonborrowed reserves was based on the FOMC's objectives for M1. If M1 grew faster than the objective, required reserves, which were linked to M1 through the required reserve ratios, would expand more quickly than nonborrowed reserves. With the fixed supply of nonborrowed reserves falling short of demand, banks would bid up the federal funds rate, sometimes sharply. The rise in short-term interest rates would eventually damp M1 growth, and M1 would be brought back toward its targeted path.

By late 1982, it had become clear that the combination of interest rate deregulation and financial innovation had weakened the historical link between M1 and the economic objectives of monetary policy. The FOMC began to make more discretionary decisions about money market conditions, using a wider array of economic and financial variables to judge the need for adjustments in short-term interest rates. In the day-to-day implementation of open market operations, this change was manifested in a shift of focus from a nonborrowed-reserve target to a borrowed-reserve target. The Federal Reserve routinely supplied fewer nonborrowed reserves than the estimated demand for total reserves, thus forcing depository institutions to meet their remaining need for reserves by borrowing at the discount window. The total amount borrowed was limited, however, even though the discount rate was generally below the federal funds rate, because access to discount window credit was restricted. In particular, depository institutions were required to pursue all other reasonably available sources of funds, including those available in the federal funds market, before credit was granted. During the time it was targeting borrowed reserves, the Federal Reserve influenced the level of the federal funds rate by controlling the extent to which depository institutions had to turn to the discount window. When it wanted to ease monetary policy, it would reduce the borrowed-reserve target and supply more nonborrowed reserves to meet estimated demand. With less pressure to borrow from the discount window, depository institutions would bid less aggressively for balances at the Federal Reserve and the federal funds rate would fall.

Beginning in the mid-1980s, spreading doubts about the financial health of some depository institutions led to an increasing reluctance on the part of many institutions to borrow at the discount window, thus weakening the link between borrowing and the federal funds rate. Consequently, the Federal Reserve increasingly sought to attain a specific level of the federal funds rate rather than a targeted amount of borrowed reserves. In July 1995, the FOMC began to announce its target for the federal funds rate.

In the federal funds market, depository institutions actively trade balances held at the Federal Reserve with each other, usually overnight, on an uncollateralized basis. Institutions with surplus balances in their accounts lend those balances to institutions in need of larger balances. The federal funds rate—the interest rate at which these transactions occur—is an important benchmark in financial markets. Daily fluctuations in the federal funds rate reflect demand and supply conditions in the market for Federal Reserve balances.

Demand for Federal Reserve Balances

The demand for Federal Reserve balances has three components: required reserve balances, contractual clearing balances, and excess reserve balances.

Required Reserve Balances

Required reserve balances are balances that a depository institution must hold with the Federal Reserve to satisfy its reserve requirement. Reserve requirements are imposed on all depository institutions—which include commercial banks, savings banks, savings and loan associations, and credit unions—as well as U.S. branches and agencies of foreign banks and other

The Market for Balances at the Federal Reserve

Securities portfolio
- holdings of U.S. Treasury securities and repurchase agreements
- purchases or sales of securities are called open market operations
- purchases increase balances

Required reserve balances
- held to satisfy reserve requirements
- do not earn interest

Contractual clearing balances
- held to meet contractually agreed-upon amount
- generate earnings credits that defray cost of Federal Reserve priced services

Loans
- credit extended to depository institutions through discount window
- making a loan increases balances

Autonomous factors
- other items on the Federal Reserve's balance sheet such as Federal Reserve notes, Treasury's balance at the Federal Reserve, and Federal Reserve float
- can add or drain balances

Excess reserves
- held to provide additional protection against overnight overdrafts and reserve or clearing balance deficiencies

DEMAND

SUPPLY

domestic banking entities that engage in international transactions. Since the early 1990s, reserve requirements have been applied only to transaction deposits, which include demand deposits and interest-bearing accounts that offer unlimited checking privileges. An institution's reserve requirement is a fraction of such deposits; the fraction—the required reserve ratio—is set by the Board of Governors within limits prescribed in the Federal Reserve Act. A depository institution's reserve requirement expands or contracts with the level of its transaction deposits and with the required reserve ratio set by the Board. In practice, the changes in required reserves reflect movements in transaction deposits because the Federal Reserve adjusts the required reserve ratio only infrequently.

A depository institution satisfies its reserve requirement by its holdings of vault cash (currency in its vault) and, if vault cash is insufficient to meet the requirement, by the balance maintained directly with a Federal Reserve Bank or indirectly with a pass-through correspondent bank (which in turn holds the balances in its account at the Federal Reserve). The difference between an institution's reserve requirement and the vault cash used to meet that requirement is called the required reserve balance. If the balance maintained by the depository institution does not satisfy its reserve balance requirement, the deficiency may be subject to a charge.

Contractual Clearing Balances

Depository institutions use their accounts at Federal Reserve Banks not only to satisfy their reserve balance requirements but also to clear many financial transactions. Given the volume and unpredictability of transactions that clear through their accounts every day, depository institutions seek to hold an end-of-day balance that is high enough to protect against unexpected debits that could leave their accounts overdrawn at the end of the day and against any resulting charges, which could be quite large. If a depository institution finds that targeting an end-of-day balance equal to its required reserve balance provides insufficient protection against overdrafts, it may establish a contractual clearing balance (sometimes referred to as a required clearing balance).

A contractual clearing balance is an amount that a depository institution agrees to hold at its Reserve Bank in addition to any required reserve balance. In return, the depository institution earns implicit interest, in the form of earnings credits, on the balance held to satisfy its contractual clearing balance. It uses these credits to defray the cost of the Federal Reserve services it uses, such as check clearing and wire transfers of funds and securities. If the depository institution fails to satisfy its contractual requirement, the deficiency is subject to a charge.

Excess Reserve Balances

A depository institution may hold balances at its Federal Reserve Bank in addition to those it must hold to meet its reserve balance requirement and its contractual clearing balance; these balances are called excess reserve balances (or excess reserves). In general, a depository institution attempts to keep excess reserve balances at low levels because balances at the Federal Reserve do not earn interest. However, a depository institution may aim to hold some positive excess reserve balances at the end of the day as additional protection against an overnight overdraft in its account or the risk of failing to hold enough balances to satisfy its reserve or clearing balance requirement. This desired cushion of balances can vary considerably from day to day, depending in part on the volume and uncertainty about payments flowing through the institution's account. The daily demand for excess reserve balances is the least-predictable component of the demand for balances. (See table 3.1 for data on required reserve balances, contractual clearing balances, and excess reserve balances.)

Purchases or sales of securities by the Federal Reserve, whether outright or temporary, are called open market operations.

Table 3.1

Measures of aggregate balances, 2001–2004
Billions of dollars; annual averages of daily data

Year	Required reserve balances	Contractual clearing balances	Excess reserve balances
2001	7.2	7.0	2.8
2002	8.0	9.7	1.5
2003	10.0	11.0	1.8
2004	11.0	10.4	1.6

Supply of Federal Reserve Balances

The supply of Federal Reserve balances to depository institutions comes from three sources: the Federal Reserve's portfolio of securities and repurchase agreements; loans from the Federal Reserve through its discount window facility; and certain other items on the Federal Reserve's balance sheet known as autonomous factors.

Securities Portfolio

The most important source of balances to depository institutions is the Federal Reserve's portfolio of securities. The Federal Reserve buys and sells securities either on an outright (also called permanent) basis or temporarily in the form of repurchase agreements and reverse repurchase agreements. Purchases or sales of securities by the Federal Reserve, whether outright or temporary, are called open market operations, and they are the Federal Reserve's principal tool for influencing the supply of balances at the Federal Reserve Banks. Open market operations are conducted to align the supply of balances at the Federal Reserve with the demand for those balances at the target rate set by the FOMC.

Purchasing securities or arranging a repurchase agreement increases the quantity of balances because the Federal Reserve creates balances when it credits the account of the seller's depository institution at the Federal Reserve for the amount of the transaction; there is no corresponding offset in another institution's account. Conversely, selling securities or conducting a reverse repurchase agreement decreases the quantity of Federal Reserve balances because the Federal Reserve extinguishes balances when it debits the account of the purchaser's depository institution at the Federal Reserve; there is no corresponding increase in another institution's account. In contrast, when financial institutions, business firms, or individuals buy or sell securities among themselves, the credit to the account of the seller's depository institution is offset by the debit to the account of the purchaser's depository institution; so existing balances held at the Federal Reserve are redistributed from one depository institution to another without changing the total available.

Discount Window Lending

The supply of Federal Reserve balances increases when depository institutions borrow from the Federal Reserve's discount window.

The supply of Federal Reserve balances increases when depository institutions borrow from the Federal Reserve's discount window. Access to discount window credit is established by rules set by the Board of Governors, and loans are made at interest rates set by the Reserve Banks and approved by the Board. Depository institutions decide to borrow based on the level of the lending rate and their liquidity needs. Beginning in early 2003, rates for discount window loans have been set above prevailing market rates (see "Major Revision to Discount Window Programs" on page 47). As a result, depository institutions typically will borrow from the discount window in significant volume only when overall market conditions have tightened enough to push the federal funds rate up close to the discount rate. Overall market conditions tend to tighten to such an extent only infrequently, so the volume of balances supplied through the discount window is usually only a small portion of the total supply of Federal Reserve balances. However, at times of market disruptions, such as after the terrorist attacks in 2001, loans extended through the discount window can supply a considerable volume of Federal Reserve balances.

Autonomous Factors

The supply of balances can vary substantially from day to day because of movements in other items on the Federal Reserve's balance sheet (table

3.2). These so-called autonomous factors are generally outside the Federal Reserve's direct day-to-day control. The most important of these factors are Federal Reserve notes, the Treasury's balance at the Federal Reserve, and Federal Reserve float.

The largest autonomous factor is Federal Reserve notes. When a depository institution needs currency, it places an order with a Federal Reserve Bank. When the Federal Reserve fills the order, it debits the account of the depository institution at the Federal Reserve, and total Federal Reserve balances decline. The amount of currency demanded tends to grow over time, in part reflecting increases in nominal spending as the economy grows. Consequently, an increasing volume of balances would be extinguished, and the federal funds rate would rise, if the Federal Reserve did not offset the contraction in balances by purchasing securities. Indeed, the expansion of Federal Reserve notes is the primary reason that the Federal Reserve's holdings of securities grow over time.

Table 3.2

Consolidated balance sheet of the Federal Reserve Banks, December 31, 2004

Millions of dollars

Assets		Liabilities	
Securities	717,819	Federal Reserve notes	719,436
Repurchase agreements	33,000	Reverse repurchase agreements	30,783
Loans	43	Balance, U.S. Treasury account	5,912
Float	927	Other liabilities and capital	27,745
All other assets	56,130	Balances, all depository institutions	24,043

Another important factor is the balance in the U.S. Treasury's account at the Federal Reserve. The Treasury draws on this account to make payments by check or direct deposit for all types of federal spending. When these payments clear, the Treasury's account is reduced and the account of the depository institution for the person or entity that receives the funds is increased. The Treasury is not a depository institution, so a payment by the Treasury to the public (for example, a Social Security payment) raises the volume of Federal Reserve balances available to depository institutions. Movements in the Treasury's balance at the Federal Reserve tend to be less predictable following corporate and individual tax dates, especially in the weeks following the April 15 deadline for federal income tax payments.

Federal Reserve float is created when the account of the depository institution presenting a check for payment is credited on a different day than the account of the depository institution on which the check is drawn is debited. This situation can arise because credit is granted to the presenting depository institution on a preset schedule, whereas the paying institution's account is not debited until the check is presented to it. Float temporarily adds Federal Reserve balances when there is a delay in debiting the paying institution's account because the two depository institutions essentially are credited with the same balances. Float temporarily drains balances when the paying institution's account is debited before the presenting institution receives credit under the schedule. Float tends to be quite high and variable following inclement weather that disrupts the normal check-delivery process.

Controlling the Federal Funds Rate

The Federal Reserve's conduct of open market operations, its policies related to required reserves and contractual clearing balances, and its lending through the discount window all play important roles in keeping the federal funds rate close to the FOMC's target rate. Open market operations are the most powerful and often-used tool for controlling the funds rate. These operations, which are arranged nearly every business day, are designed to bring the supply of Federal Reserve balances in line with the demand for those balances at the FOMC's target rate. Required reserve balances and contractual clearing balances facilitate the conduct of open market operations by creating a predictable demand for Federal Reserve balances. If, even after an open market operation is arranged, the supply of balances falls short of demand, then discount window lending provides a mechanism for expanding the supply of balances to contain pressures on the funds rate.

Open market operations are the most powerful and often-used tool for controlling the federal funds rate.

Reserve balance requirements and contractual clearing balances need to be met only on average over a so-called reserve maintenance period, not each day. This structure gives depository institutions considerable flexibility in managing their end-of-day balances at the Federal Reserve from one day to the next. This flexibility helps smooth fluctuations in the federal funds rate. If a depository institution finds that its balance at the Federal Reserve is unexpectedly high on one day (for instance, because a customer made an unexpected deposit or an expected payment was not made), it does not have to offer to lend the extra balance at very low rates; it can absorb the surplus by choosing to hold lower balances in the remaining days of the maintenance period and still meet its balance requirements. Holding a lower balance on a subsequent day of the period does not necessarily increase the likelihood that the depository institution will incur an overnight overdraft if the sum of its required reserve balance and contractual clearing balance is high relative to its payment needs. This flexibility in managing account balances protects against variations in the demand for and supply of Federal Reserve balances that would otherwise put pressure on the federal funds rate.

Reserve balance requirements and contractual clearing balances also help create a predictable demand for balances at the Federal Reserve. Without reserve balance requirements or contractual clearing balances, many depository institutions would still hold positive balances at the Federal Reserve to facilitate payments on behalf of themselves or their customers and to avoid having a negative balance in their account at the end of the day. The exact amount of balances that depository institutions want to hold at the Federal Reserve at the end of the day for clearing purposes can vary considerably from day to day, often depending on the volume and uncertainty of the payment flows through their accounts. These demands are very difficult for the Federal Reserve to forecast. When the level of reserve balance requirements, contractual clearing balances, or the sum of the two make it necessary for depository institutions to hold balances above the shifting and unpredictable level needed for clearing purposes, the Federal Reserve can more accurately determine the demand for Federal Reserve balances and, by manipulating the supply of Federal Reserve balances through open market operations, more readily attain the target funds rate.

The remainder of this chapter takes a more detailed look at open market operations, reserve requirements, contractual clearing balances, and the discount window.

Open Market Operations

In theory, the Federal Reserve could conduct open market operations by purchasing or selling any type of asset. In practice, however, most assets cannot be traded readily enough to accommodate open market operations. For open market operations to work effectively, the Federal Reserve must be able to buy and sell quickly, at its own convenience, in whatever volume may be needed to keep the federal funds rate at the target level. These conditions require that the instrument it buys or sells be traded in a broad, highly active market that can accommodate the transactions without distortions or disruptions to the market itself.

The market for U.S. Treasury securities satisfies these conditions. The U.S. Treasury securities market is the broadest and most active of U.S. financial markets. Transactions are handled over the counter, not on an organized exchange. Although most of the trading occurs in New York City, telephone and computer connections link dealers, brokers, and customers—regardless of their location—to form a global market.

Composition of the Federal Reserve's Portfolio

The overall size of the Federal Reserve's holdings of Treasury securities depends principally on the growth of Federal Reserve notes; however, the amounts and maturities of the individual securities held depends on the FOMC's preferences for liquidity. The Federal Reserve has guidelines that limit its holdings of individual Treasury securities to a percentage of the total amount outstanding. These guidelines are designed to help the Federal Reserve manage the liquidity and average maturity of the System portfolio. The percentage limits under these guidelines are larger for shorter-dated issues than longer-dated ones. Consequently, a sizable share of the Federal Reserve's holdings is held in Treasury securities with remaining maturities of one year or less. This structure provides the Federal Reserve with the ability to alter the composition of its assets quickly when developments warrant. At the end of 2004, the Federal Reserve's holdings of Treasury securities were about evenly weighted between those with maturities of one year or less and those with maturities greater than one year (table 3.3).

Table 3.3

U.S. Treasury securities held in the Federal Reserve's open market account, December 31, 2004
Billions of dollars

Remaining maturity	U.S. Treasury securities
1 year or less	379.4
More than 1 year to 5 years	208.3
More than 5 years to 10 years	54.4
More than 10 years	75.8
Total	717.8

The Conduct of Open Market Operations

The Federal Reserve Bank of New York conducts open market operations for the Federal Reserve, under an authorization from the Federal Open Market Committee. The group that carries out the operations is commonly referred to as "the Open Market Trading Desk" or "the Desk." The Desk is permitted by the FOMC's authorization to conduct business with U.S. securities dealers and with foreign official and international institutions that maintain accounts at the Federal Reserve Bank of New York. The dealers with which the Desk transacts business are called primary dealers. The Federal Reserve requires primary dealers to meet the capital standards of their primary regulators and satisfy other criteria consistent with being a meaningful and creditworthy counterparty. All open market operations transacted with primary dealers are conducted through an auction process.

Each day, the Desk must decide whether to conduct open market operations, and, if so, the types of operations to conduct. It examines forecasts of the daily supply of Federal Reserve balances from autonomous factors and discount window lending. The forecasts, which extend several weeks into the future, assume that the Federal Reserve abstains from open market operations. These forecasts are compared with projections of the demand for balances to determine the need for open market operations. The decision about the types of operations to conduct depends on how long a deficiency or surplus of Federal Reserve balances is expected to last. If staff projections indicate that the demand for balances is likely to exceed the supply of balances by a large amount for a number of weeks or months, the Federal Reserve may make outright purchases of securities or arrange longer-term repurchase agreements to increase supply. Conversely, if the projections suggest that demand is likely to fall short of supply, then the Federal Reserve may sell securities outright or redeem maturing securities to shrink the supply of balances.

Even after accounting for planned outright operations or long-term repurchase agreements, there may still be a short-term need to alter Federal Reserve balances. In these circumstances, the Desk assesses whether the federal funds rate is likely to remain near the FOMC's target rate in light of the estimated imbalance between supply and demand. If the funds rate is likely to move away from the target rate, then the Desk will arrange short-term repurchase agreements, which add balances, or reverse repurchase agreements, which drain balances, to better align the supply of and demand for balances. If the funds rate is likely to remain close to the target, then the Desk will not arrange a short-term operation. Short-term temporary operations are much more common than outright transactions because daily fluctuations in autonomous factors or the demand for excess reserve balances can create a sizable imbalance between the supply of and demand for balances that might cause the federal funds rate to move significantly away from the FOMC's target.

Outright Purchases and Sales

The Federal Reserve tends to conduct far more outright purchases than outright sales or redemptions of securities primarily because it must offset the drain of balances resulting from the public's increasing demand for Federal Reserve notes (table 3.4). When the Desk decides to buy securities in an outright operation, it first determines how much it wants to buy to address the mismatch between supply and demand. It then divides that amount into smaller portions and makes a series of purchases in different segments of the maturity spectrum, rather than buying securities across all maturities at once, in order to minimize the impact on market prices.

When the projections indicate a need to drain Federal Reserve balances, the Desk may choose to sell securities or to redeem maturing securities. Sales of securities are extremely rare. By redeeming some maturing securities, rather than exchanging all of them for new issues, the Federal Reserve can reduce the size of its holdings gradually without having to enter the market. Redemptions drain Federal Reserve balances when the Treasury takes funds out of its accounts at depository institutions, transfers those funds to its account at the Federal Reserve, and then pays the Federal Reserve for the maturing issues.

Table 3.4

Federal Reserve System outright transactions, 2001–2004

Billions of dollars

Transaction	2001	2002	2003	2004
Purchases	68.5	54.2	36.8	50.5
Redemptions	26.9	—	—	—
Total	95.4	54.2	36.8	50.5

Purchases from and sales to foreign official and international customers enable the Federal Reserve to make small adjustments to its portfolio without formally entering the market. These transactions occur at market prices. The size of the buy or sell orders of these customers and the projected need for open market operations determine whether the Desk chooses to arrange these customer transactions directly with the Federal Reserve, in which case they affect Federal Reserve balances, or to act as agent by conducting the transactions in the market, with no effect on balances.

Repurchase Agreements

The Federal Reserve frequently arranges repurchase agreements to add Federal Reserve balances temporarily (table 3.5). In these transactions, it acquires a security from a primary dealer under an agreement to return the security on a specified date. Most repurchase agreements have an overnight term, although short-term repurchase agreements with maturities of two to thirteen days are also arranged to address shortages in Federal Reserve balances that are expected to extend over several days. Longer-term repurchase agreements are used to address more-persistent needs. The Federal Reserve accepts Treasury, federal agency, and mortgage-backed securities guaranteed by federal agencies as collateral for its repurchase agreements.

Table 3.5

Federal Reserve System temporary transactions, 2001–2004

Volume in billions of dollars

	2001		2002		2003		2004	
	Num.	Vol.	Num.	Vol.	Num.	Vol.	Num.	Vol.
Repurchase agreements[1]	305	1,497.7	262	1,143.1	288	1,522.9	299	1,876.9
Matched sale–purchase transactions/ Reverse repurchase agreements[2]	10	25.0	7	11.3	10	22.8	2	4.8

1. Includes all types of repurchase agreements.
2. Reverse repurchase agreements after 2003.

Reverse Repurchase Agreements

When the Federal Reserve needs to absorb Federal Reserve balances temporarily, it enters into reverse repurchase agreements with primary dealers. These transactions involve selling a Treasury security to a primary dealer under an agreement to receive the security back on a specified date. As in repurchase agreement transactions, these operations are arranged on an auction basis. When the Federal Reserve transfers the collateral (usually a Treasury bill) to the dealer, the account of the dealer's clearing bank at the Federal Reserve is debited, and total Federal Reserve balances decline. When the transaction unwinds, the account of the dealer's clearing bank is credited and total balances increase.

Every business day, the Federal Reserve also arranges reverse repurchase agreements with foreign official and international accounts. These institutions have accounts at the Federal Reserve Bank of New York to help manage their U.S. dollar payments and receipts. The Federal Reserve permits these institutions to invest cash balances overnight through these agreements.

A Typical Day in the Conduct of Open Market Operations

Each weekday, beginning at around 7:30 a.m., two groups of Federal Reserve staff members, one at the Federal Reserve Bank of New York and one at the Board of Governors in Washington, prepare independent projections of the supply of and demand for Federal Reserve balances.

The manager of the System Open Market Account and the group in New York are linked in a telephone conference call with members of the staff at the Board of Governors and with a Federal Reserve Bank president who is currently a member of the FOMC. Participants in the call discuss staff forecasts for Federal Reserve balances and recent developments in financial markets. They pay special attention to trading conditions in the federal funds market, particularly the level of the federal funds rate in relation to the FOMC's target. In light of this information, they determine a plan for open market operations. The decision is announced to the markets at around 9:30 a.m., at the same time that the Desk solicits offers from dealers. (Typically, longer-term repurchase agreements are arranged earlier in the morning, usually on a specific day of the week.) If an outright operation is also needed, it would typically be executed later in the morning, after the daily operation is complete.

Securities Lending

The Federal Reserve has a securities lending program designed to provide a secondary and temporary source of securities to the market in order to promote the smooth clearing of Treasury securities. Under this program, securities from the portfolio are offered for loan to primary dealers through an auction process each day at noon. The total amount available for an individual security is a fraction of the Federal Reserve's total holdings, and there are limits on the amount of securities that can be lent to a single dealer. As collateral, the dealer gives the Federal Reserve other securities, not cash; therefore, the Federal Reserve's lending operations do not affect the supply of Federal Reserve balances and are not considered open market operations.

Reserve Requirements

Reserve requirements have long been a part of our nation's banking history. Depository institutions maintain a fraction of certain liabilities in reserve in specified assets. The Federal Reserve can adjust reserve requirements by changing required reserve ratios, the liabilities to which the ratios apply, or both. Changes in reserve requirements can have profound effects on the money stock and on the cost to banks of extending credit and are also costly to administer; therefore, reserve requirements are not adjusted frequently. Nonetheless, reserve requirements play a useful role in the conduct of open market operations by helping to ensure a predictable demand for Federal Reserve balances and thus enhancing the Federal Reserve's control over the federal funds rate.

Requiring depository institutions to hold a certain fraction of their deposits in reserve, either as cash in their vaults or as non-interest-bearing

Reserve requirements play a useful role in the conduct of open market operations by helping to ensure a predictable demand for Federal Reserve balances.

balances at the Federal Reserve, does impose a cost on the private sector. The cost is equal to the amount of forgone interest on these funds—or at least on the portion of these funds that depository institutions hold only because of legal requirements and not to meet their customers' needs.

The burden of reserve requirements is structured to bear generally less heavily on smaller institutions. At every depository institution, a certain amount of reservable liabilities is exempt from reserve requirements, and a relatively low required reserve ratio is applied to reservable liabilities up to a specific level. The amounts of reservable liabilities exempt from reserve requirements and subject to the low required reserve ratio are adjusted annually to reflect growth in the banking system. Table 3.6 shows the reserve requirement ratios in effect in 2004.

Table 3.6

Reserve requirement ratios, 2004

The burden of reserve requirements is structured to bear generally less heavily on smaller institutions.

Category	Reserve requirement
Net transaction accounts	
$0 to $6.6 million	0 percent of amount
Over $6.6 million and up to $45.4 million	3 percent of amount
Over $45.4 million	$1,164,000 plus 10 percent of amount over $45.4 million
Nonpersonal time deposits	0 percent
Eurocurrency liabilities	0 percent

Changes in reserve requirements can affect the money stock, by altering the volume of deposits that can be supported by a given level of reserves, and bank funding costs. Unless it is accompanied by an increase in the supply of Federal Reserve balances, an increase in reserve requirements (through an increase in the required reserve ratio, for example) reduces excess reserves, induces a contraction in bank credit and deposit levels, and raises interest rates. It also pushes up bank funding costs by increasing the amount of non-interest-bearing assets that must be held in reserve. Conversely, a decrease in reserve requirements, unless accompanied by a reduction in Federal Reserve balances, initially leaves depository institutions with excess reserves, which can encourage an expansion of bank credit and deposit levels and reduce interest rates.

Recent History of Reserve Requirements

In the 1960s and 1970s, the Federal Reserve actively used reserve requirements as a tool of monetary policy in order to influence the expansion of money and credit partly by manipulating bank funding costs. As financial innovation spawned new sources of bank funding, the Federal Reserve adapted reserve requirements to these new financial products. It changed required reserve ratios on specific bank liabilities that were most frequently used to fund new lending. Reserve requirements were also imposed on other, newly emerging liabilities that were the functional equivalents of deposits, such as Eurodollar borrowings. At times, it supplemented these actions by placing a marginal reserve requirement on large time deposits —that is, an additional requirement applied only to each new increment of these deposits.

As the 1970s unfolded, it became increasingly apparent that the structure of reserve requirements was becoming outdated. At this time, only banks that were members of the Federal Reserve System were subject to reserve requirements established by the Federal Reserve. The regulatory structure and competitive pressures during a period of high interest rates were putting an increasing burden on member banks. This situation fostered the growth of deposits, especially the newly introduced interest-bearing transaction deposits, at institutions other than member banks and led many banks to leave the Federal Reserve System. Given this situation, policy makers felt that reserve requirements needed to be applied to a broad group of institutions for more effective monetary control—that is, to strengthen the relationship between the amount of reserves supplied by the Federal Reserve and the overall quantity of money in the economy.

Changes in reserve requirements can affect the money stock and bank funding costs.

The Monetary Control Act of 1980 (MCA) ended the problem of membership attrition and facilitated monetary control by reforming reserve requirements. Under the act, all depository institutions are subject to reserve requirements set by the Federal Reserve, whether or not they are members of the Federal Reserve System. The Board of Governors may impose reserve requirements solely for the purpose of implementing monetary policy. The required reserve ratio may range from 8 percent to 14 percent on transaction deposits and from 0 percent to 9 percent on nonpersonal time deposits. The Board may also set reserve requirements on the net liabilities owed by depository institutions in the United States to their foreign affiliates or to other foreign banks. The MCA permits the Board, under certain circumstances, to establish supplemental and emergency reserve requirements, but these powers have never been exercised.

Following the passage of the MCA in 1980, reserve requirements were not adjusted for policy purposes for a decade. In December 1990, the required reserve ratio on nonpersonal time deposits was pared from 3 percent to 0 percent, and in April 1992 the 12 percent ratio on transaction deposits was trimmed to 10 percent. These actions were partly motivated by evidence suggesting that some lenders had adopted a more cautious approach to extending credit, which was increasing the cost and restricting the availability of credit to some types of borrowers. By reducing funding costs and thus providing depository institutions with easier access to capital markets, the cuts in required reserve ratios put depository institutions in a better position to extend credit.

Although reserve requirement ratios have not been changed since the early 1990s, the level of reserve requirements and required reserve balances has fallen considerably since then because of the widespread implementation of retail sweep programs by depository institutions. Under such a program, a depository institution sweeps amounts above a predetermined level from a depositor's checking account into a special-purpose money market deposit account created for the depositor. In this way, the depository institution shifts funds from an account that is subject to reserve requirements to one that is not and therefore reduces its reserve requirement. With no change in its vault cash holdings, the depository institution can lower its required reserve balance, on which it earns no interest, and invest the funds formerly held at the Federal Reserve in interest-earning assets.

Contractual Clearing Balances

Contractual clearing balances, like required reserve balances, help to create a stable, predictable demand for Federal Reserve balances, which assists in the conduct of open market operations. In early 1981, the Federal Reserve Board established a policy that permitted all depository institutions to hold contractual clearing balances at the Federal Reserve Banks. Such balances, which were referred to as required clearing balances at the time, were established following the passage of the MCA to facilitate access to Federal Reserve priced services by depository institutions with zero or low required reserve balances. Use of these arrangements was minimal in the early 1980s because required reserve balances were sufficiently high to facilitate clearing and meet reserve requirements.

Chart 3.1
Balances at Federal Reserve Banks, 1990–2004
Monthly $ Billions

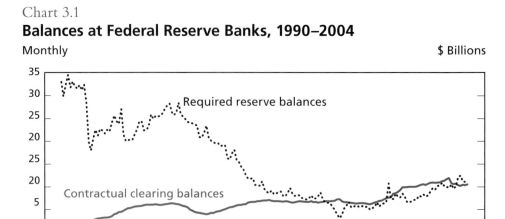

The use of contractual clearing balances rose considerably in the 1990s as required reserve balances dropped in the wake of the cuts in required reserve ratios early in the decade and the widespread implementation of retail sweep programs by depository institutions. The resulting reduction in required reserve balances left some depository institutions with insufficient protection against overnight overdrafts, so they established or expanded their contractual clearing balances. The rise in contractual clearing balances during the 1990s did not match the decline in required reserve balances, however, in part because depository institutions apparently did not need as large a cushion to protect against overnight overdrafts as was once provided by their required reserve balance. In addition, the ability of some depository institutions to expand their contractual clearing balances was limited by the extent to which they use Federal Reserve priced services.

The Discount Window

The Federal Reserve's lending at the discount window serves two primary functions. It complements open market operations in achieving the target federal funds rate by making Federal Reserve balances available to depository institutions when the supply of balances falls short of demand. It also serves as a backup source of liquidity for individual depository institutions.

At times when the normal functioning of financial markets is disrupted, the discount window can become the principal channel for supplying balances to depository institutions.

FEDERAL RESERVE press release

For immediate release   September 11, 2001

    The Federal Reserve System is open and operating. The
discount window is available to meet liquidity needs.
                          -0-

Although the volume of discount window borrowing is relatively small, it plays an important role in containing upward pressures on the federal funds rate. If a depository institution faces an unexpectedly low balance in its account at the Federal Reserve, either because the total supply of balances has fallen short of demand or because it failed to receive an expected transfer of funds from a counterparty, it can borrow at the discount window. This extension of credit increases the supply of Federal

Reserve balances and helps to limit any upward pressure on the federal funds rate. At times when the normal functioning of financial markets is disrupted—for example after operational problems, a natural disaster, or a terrorist attack—the discount window can become the principal channel for supplying balances to depository institutions.

The discount window can also, at times, serve as a useful tool for promoting financial stability by providing temporary funding to depository institutions that are having significant financial difficulties. If the institution's sudden collapse were likely to have severe adverse effects on the financial system, an extension of central bank credit could be desirable because it would address the liquidity strains and permit the institution to make a transition to sounder footing. Discount window credit can also be used to facilitate an orderly resolution of a failing institution. An institution obtaining credit in either situation must be monitored appropriately to ensure that it does not take excessive risks in an attempt to return to profitability and that the use of central bank credit would not increase costs to the deposit insurance fund and ultimately the taxpayer.

Types of Credit

In ordinary circumstances, the Federal Reserve extends discount window credit to depository institutions under the primary, secondary, and seasonal credit programs. The rates charged on loans under each of these programs are established by each Reserve Bank's board of directors every two weeks, subject to review and determination by the Board of Governors. The rates for each of the three lending programs are the same at all Reserve Banks, except occasionally for very brief periods following the Board's action to adopt a requested rate change. The Federal Reserve also has the authority under the Federal Reserve Act to extend credit to entities that are not depository institutions in "unusual and exigent circumstances"; however, such lending has not occurred since the 1930s.

Primary Credit

Primary credit is available to generally sound depository institutions on a very short-term basis, typically overnight. To assess whether a depository institution is in sound financial condition, its Reserve Bank regularly reviews the institution's condition, using supervisory ratings and data on adequacy of the institution's capital. Depository institutions are not required to seek alternative sources of funds before requesting occasional advances of primary credit, but primary credit is expected to be used as a backup, rather than a regular, source of funding.

The rate on primary credit has typically been set 1 percentage point above the FOMC's target federal funds rate, but the spread can vary depending on circumstances. Because primary credit is the Federal Reserve's main dis-

Major Revision to Discount Window Programs

On January 9, 2003, the Federal Reserve significantly revised its discount window lending programs, replacing the previous adjustment and extended credit programs with primary and secondary credit facilities. Adjustment credit had been made available to help depository institutions make short-term balance-sheet adjustments and to provide an alternate source of funds in the event of a shortfall in the supply of Federal Reserve balances. Extended credit, which was intended to accommodate depository institutions' somewhat longer-term liquidity needs resulting from exceptional circumstances, had not been used since 1995.

Adjustment credit was extended at the basic discount rate, which over the previous decade had been 25 to 50 basis points below the usual level of overnight market interest rates. The below-market interest rate on adjustment credit had caused several significant problems. The incentive for depository institutions to exploit the below-market rate meant that borrowing requests necessarily were subject to considerable administration by Reserve Banks. In particular, borrowers were required to seek funds elsewhere before coming to the window. Partly as a result of those requirements, many depository institutions were reluctant to borrow from the discount window, reducing the effectiveness of the discount window in buffering shocks to the money market.

Under the revised lending programs, the above-market rate and the fact that primary credit is restricted to financially sound institutions mean that primary credit can be extended largely without administration, making depository institutions more willing to borrow and so making the discount window a more effective monetary policy tool. The central banks of nearly all industrialized countries have similar lending facilities that extend collateralized credit at an above-market rate with little or no administration.

Chart 3.3

Effective federal funds rate and discount rate, 1955–2004*

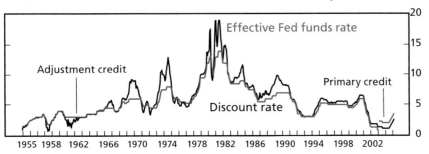

* On January 9, 2003, the main discount rate switched from being the rate on adjustment credit to the rate on primary credit.

count window program, the Federal Reserve at times uses the term *discount rate* specifically to mean the primary credit rate.

Reserve Banks ordinarily do not require depository institutions to provide reasons for requesting very short-term primary credit. Borrowers are asked to provide only the minimum information necessary to process a loan, usually the requested amount and term of the loan. If a pattern of borrowing or the nature of a particular borrowing request strongly indicates that a depository institution is not generally sound or is using primary credit as a regular rather than a backup source of funding, a Reserve Bank may seek additional information before deciding whether to extend the loan.

Primary credit may be extended for longer periods of up to a few weeks if a depository institution is in generally sound financial condition and cannot obtain temporary funds in the market at reasonable terms. Large and medium-sized institutions are unlikely to meet this test.

Secondary Credit

Depository institutions that have reservable transaction accounts or nonpersonal time deposits may borrow from the discount window.

Secondary credit is available to depository institutions that are not eligible for primary credit. It is extended on a very short-term basis, typically overnight. Reflecting the less-sound financial condition of borrowers of secondary credit, the rate on secondary credit has typically been 50 basis points above the primary credit rate, although the spread can vary as circumstances warrant. Secondary credit is available to help a depository institution meet backup liquidity needs when its use is consistent with the borrowing institution's timely return to a reliance on market sources of funding or with the orderly resolution of a troubled institution's difficulties. Secondary credit may not be used to fund an expansion of the borrower's assets.

Loans extended under the secondary credit program entail a higher level of Reserve Bank administration and oversight than loans under the primary credit program. A Reserve Bank must have sufficient information about a borrower's financial condition and reasons for borrowing to ensure that an extension of secondary credit would be consistent with the purpose of the facility. Moreover, under the Federal Deposit Insurance Corporation Improvement Act of 1991, extensions of Federal Reserve credit to an FDIC-insured depository institution that has fallen below minimum capital standards are generally limited to 60 days in any 120-day period or, for the most severely undercapitalized, to only five days.

Seasonal Credit

The Federal Reserve's seasonal credit program is designed to help small depository institutions manage significant seasonal swings in their loans and deposits. Seasonal credit is available to depository institutions that can demonstrate a clear pattern of recurring swings in funding needs throughout the year—usually institutions in agricultural or tourist areas. Borrowing longer-term funds from the discount window during periods of seasonal need allows institutions to carry fewer liquid assets during the rest of the year and make more funds available for local lending.

The seasonal credit rate is based on market interest rates. It is set on the first business day of each two-week reserve maintenance period as the average of the effective federal funds rate and the interest rate on three-month certificates of deposit over the previous reserve maintenance period.

Eligibility to Borrow

By law, depository institutions that have reservable transaction accounts or nonpersonal time deposits may borrow from the discount window. U.S. branches and agencies of foreign banks that are subject to reserve requirements are eligible to borrow under the same general terms and conditions that apply to domestic depository institutions. Banker's banks, corporate credit unions, and certain other banking institutions that are not subject to reserve requirements generally do not have access to the discount window. However, the Board of Governors has determined that those institutions may obtain access to the discount window if they voluntarily maintain required reserve balances.

Chart 3.2
Collateral value by asset type, December 31, 2004

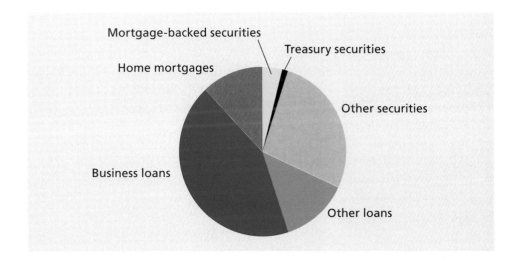

Discount Window Collateral

By law, all discount window loans must be secured by collateral to the satisfaction of the lending Reserve Bank. Most loans that are not past due and most investment-grade securities held by depository institutions are acceptable as collateral. Reserve Banks must be able to establish a legal right in the event of default to be first in line to take possession of and, if necessary, sell all collateral that secures discount window loans.

Reserve Banks assign a lendable value to assets accepted as collateral. The lendable value is the maximum loan amount that can be backed by that asset. It is based on market values, if available, or par values—in both cases reduced by a margin. The margin depends on how accurately the asset can be valued, how much its value tends to vary over time, the liquidity of the asset, and the financial condition of the pledging institution.

4 The Federal Reserve in the International Sphere

The U.S. economy and the world economy are linked in many ways. Economic developments in this country have a major influence on production, employment, and prices beyond our borders; at the same time, developments abroad significantly affect our economy. The U.S. dollar, which is the currency most used in international transactions, constitutes more than half of other countries' official foreign exchange reserves. U.S. banks abroad and foreign banks in the United States are important actors in international financial markets.

The activities of the Federal Reserve and the international economy influence each other. Therefore, when deciding on the appropriate monetary policy for achieving basic economic goals, the Board of Governors and the FOMC consider the record of U.S. international transactions, movements in foreign exchange rates, and other international economic developments. And in the area of bank supervision and regulation, innovations in international banking require continual assessments of, and occasional modifications in, the Federal Reserve's procedures and regulations.

The Federal Reserve formulates policies that shape, and are shaped by, international developments. It also participates directly in international affairs. For example, the Federal Reserve occasionally undertakes foreign exchange transactions aimed at influencing the value of the dollar in relation to foreign currencies, primarily with the goal of stabilizing disorderly market conditions. These transactions are undertaken in close and continuous consultation and cooperation with the U.S. Treasury. The Federal Reserve also works with the Treasury and other government agencies on various aspects of international financial policy. It participates in a number of international organizations and forums and is in almost continuous contact with other central banks on subjects of mutual concern.

International Linkages

The Federal Reserve's actions to adjust U.S. monetary policy are designed to attain basic objectives for the U.S. economy. But any policy move also influences, and is influenced by, international developments. For example,

U.S. monetary policy actions influence exchange rates. The dollar's exchange value in terms of other currencies is therefore one of the channels through which U.S. monetary policy affects the U.S. economy. If Federal Reserve actions raised U.S. interest rates, for instance, the foreign exchange value of the dollar generally would rise. An increase in the foreign exchange value of the dollar, in turn, would raise the price in foreign currency of U.S. goods traded on world markets and lower the dollar price of goods imported into the United States. By restraining exports and boosting imports, these developments could lower output and price levels in the U.S. economy. In contrast, an increase in interest rates in a foreign country could raise worldwide demand for assets denominated in that country's currency and thereby reduce the dollar's value in terms of that currency. Other things being equal, U.S. output and price levels would tend to increase—just the opposite of what happens when U.S. interest rates rise.

Economic developments in the United States, including U.S. monetary policy actions, have significant effects on growth and inflation in foreign economies.

Therefore, when formulating monetary policy, the Board of Governors and the FOMC draw upon information about and analysis of international as well as U.S. domestic influences. Changes in public policies or in economic conditions abroad and movements in international variables that affect the U.S. economy, such as exchange rates, must be factored into the determination of U.S. monetary policy.

Conversely, economic developments in the United States, including U.S. monetary policy actions, have significant effects on growth and inflation in foreign economies. Although the Federal Reserve's policy objectives are limited to economic outcomes in the United States, it is mutually beneficial for macroeconomic and financial policy makers in the United States and other countries to maintain a continuous dialogue. This dialogue enables the Federal Reserve to better understand and anticipate influences on the U.S. economy that emanate from abroad.

The increasing complexity of global financial markets—combined with ever-increasing linkages between national markets through trade, finance, and direct investment—have led to a proliferation of forums in which policy makers from different countries can meet and discuss topics of mutual interest. One important forum is provided by the Bank for International Settlements (BIS) in Basel, Switzerland. Through the BIS, the Federal Reserve works with representatives of the central banks of other countries on mutual concerns regarding monetary policy, international financial markets, banking supervision and regulation, and payments systems. (The Chairman of the Board of Governors and the president of the Federal Reserve Board of New York represent the U.S. central bank on the board of directors of the BIS.) Representatives of the Federal Reserve also participate in the activities of the International Monetary Fund (IMF) and discuss macroeconomic, financial market, and structural issues with representatives of other industrial countries at the Organisation for Economic

Co-operation and Development (OECD). Following the Asian Financial Crises of 1997 and 1998, the Financial Stability Forum (FSF) was established to enable central banks, finance ministries, and financial regulatory authorities in systemically important economies to work together to address issues related to financial stability. The Federal Reserve also sends delegates to international meetings such as those of the Asia Pacific Economic Cooperation (APEC) Finance Ministers' Process, the G-7 Finance Ministers and Central Bank Governors, the G-20, and the Governors of Central Banks of the American Continent.

Foreign Currency Operations

The Federal Reserve conducts foreign currency operations—the buying and selling of dollars in exchange for foreign currency—under the direction of the FOMC, acting in close and continuous consultation and cooperation with the U.S. Treasury, which has overall responsibility for U.S. international financial policy. The manager of the System Open Market Account at the Federal Reserve Bank of New York acts as the agent for both the FOMC and the Treasury in carrying out foreign currency operations. Since the late 1970s, the U.S. Treasury and the Federal Reserve have conducted almost all foreign currency operations jointly and equally.

The purpose of Federal Reserve foreign currency operations has evolved in response to changes in the international monetary system. The most important of these changes was the transition in the 1970s from a system of fixed exchange rates—established in 1944 at an international monetary conference held in Bretton Woods, New Hampshire—to a system of flexible (or floating) exchange rates for the dollar in terms of other countries' currencies. Under the Bretton Woods Agreements, which created the IMF and the International Bank for Reconstruction and Development (known informally as the World Bank), foreign authorities were responsible for intervening in exchange markets to maintain their countries' exchange rates within 1 percent of their currencies' parities with the U.S. dollar; direct exchange market intervention by U.S. authorities was extremely limited. Instead, U.S. authorities were obliged to buy and sell dollars against gold to maintain the dollar price of gold near $35 per ounce. After the United States suspended the gold convertibility of the dollar in 1971, a regime of flexible exchange rates emerged; in 1973, under that regime, the United States began to intervene in exchange markets on a more significant scale. In 1978, the regime of flexible exchange rates was codified in an amendment to the IMF's Articles of Agreement.

Under flexible exchange rates, the main aim of Federal Reserve foreign currency operations has been to counter disorderly conditions in exchange markets through the purchase or sale of foreign currencies (called foreign exchange intervention operations), primarily in the New York market. During some episodes of downward pressure on the foreign exchange value of the dollar, the Federal Reserve has purchased dollars (sold foreign currency) and has thereby absorbed some of the selling pressure on the dollar. Similarly, the Federal Reserve may sell dollars (purchase foreign currency) to counter upward pressure on the dollar's foreign exchange value. The Federal Reserve Bank of New York also executes transactions in the U.S. foreign exchange market for foreign monetary authorities, using their funds.

Under flexible exchange rates, the main aim of Federal Reserve foreign currency operations has been to counter disorderly conditions in exchange markets.

In the early 1980s, the United States curtailed its official exchange market operations, although it remained ready to enter the market when necessary to counter disorderly conditions. In 1985, particularly after September, when representatives of the five major industrial countries reached the so-called Plaza Agreement on exchange rates, the United States began to use exchange market intervention as a policy instrument more frequently. Between 1985 and 1995, the Federal Reserve—sometimes in coordination with other central banks—intervened to counter dollar movements that were perceived as excessive. Based on an assessment of past experience with official intervention and a reluctance to let exchange rate issues be seen as a major focus of monetary policy, U.S. authorities have intervened only rarely since 1995.

Sterilization

Intervention operations involving dollars affect the supply of Federal Reserve balances to U.S. depository institutions, unless the Federal Reserve offsets the effect. A purchase of foreign currency by the Federal Reserve increases the supply of balances when the Federal Reserve credits the account of the seller's depository institution at the Federal Reserve. Conversely, a sale of foreign currency by the Federal Reserve decreases the supply of balances. The Federal Reserve offsets, or "sterilizes," the effects of intervention on Federal Reserve balances through open market operations; otherwise, the intervention could cause the federal funds rate to move away from the target set by the FOMC.

For example, assume that the Federal Reserve, perhaps in conjunction with Japanese authorities, wants to counter downward pressure on the dollar's foreign exchange value in relation to the Japanese yen. The Federal Reserve would sell some of its yen-denominated securities for yen on the open market and then trade the yen for dollars in the foreign exchange market, thus reducing the supply of dollar balances at the Federal Reserve. In order to sterilize the effect of intervention on the supply of Federal Reserve balances, the Open Market Desk would then purchase an equal amount of U.S. Treasury securities in the open market (or arrange a repurchase agreement), thereby raising the supply of balances back to its former level. The net effect of such an intervention is a reduction in dollar-denominated securities in the hands of the public and an increase in yen-denominated securities. The operations have no net effect on the level of yen balances at the Bank of Japan or on the level of dollar balances at the Federal Reserve.

A dollar intervention initiated by a foreign central bank also leaves the supply of balances at the Federal Reserve unaffected, unless the central bank changes the amount it has on deposit at the Federal Reserve. If, for example, the foreign central bank purchases dollars in the foreign exchange market and places them in its account at the Federal Reserve Bank of New York, then the supply of Federal Reserve balances available to U.S. depository institutions decreases because the dollars are transferred from the bank of the seller of dollars to the foreign central bank's account with the Federal Reserve. However, the Open Market Desk would offset this drain by buying a Treasury security or arranging a repurchase agreement to increase the supply of Federal Reserve balances to U.S. depository institutions. Most dollar purchases by foreign central banks are used to purchase dollar securities directly, and thus they do not need to be countered by U.S. open market operations to leave the supply of dollar balances at the Federal Reserve unchanged.

U.S. Foreign Currency Resources

The main source of foreign currencies used in U.S. intervention operations currently is U.S. holdings of foreign exchange reserves. At the end of June 2004, the United States held foreign currency reserves valued at $40 billion. Of this amount, the Federal Reserve held foreign currency assets of $20 billion, and the Exchange Stabilization Fund of the Treasury held the rest.

The U.S. monetary authorities have also arranged swap facilities with foreign monetary authorities to support foreign currency operations. These facilities, which are also known as reciprocal currency arrangements, provide short-term access to foreign currencies. A swap transaction involves both a spot (immediate delivery) transaction, in which the Federal Reserve transfers dollars to another central bank in exchange for foreign currency, and a simultaneous forward (future delivery) transaction, in which the two central banks agree to reverse the spot transaction, typically no later than three months in the future. The repurchase price incorporates a market rate of return in each currency of the transaction. The original purpose of swap arrangements was to facilitate a central bank's support of its own currency in case of undesired downward pressure in foreign exchange markets. Drawings on swap arrangements were common in the 1960s but over time declined in frequency as policy authorities came to rely more on foreign exchange reserve balances to finance currency operations.

In years past, the Federal Reserve had standing commitments to swap currencies with the central banks of more than a dozen countries. In the middle of the 1990s, these arrangements totaled more than $30 billion, but they were almost never drawn upon. At the end of 1998, these facilities were allowed to lapse by mutual agreement among the central banks involved, with the exception of arrangements with the central banks of Canada and Mexico (see table 4.1).

Reciprocal currency arrangements can be an important policy tool in times of unusual market disruptions. For example, immediately after the terrorist attacks of September 11, 2001, the Federal Reserve established temporary swap arrangements with the European Central Bank and the Bank of England, as well as a temporary augmentation of the existing arrangement with the Bank of Canada (see table 4.1). The purpose of these arrangements was to enable the foreign central banks to lend dollars to local financial institutions to facilitate the settlement of their dollar obligations and to guard against possible disruptions to the global payments system. The European Central Bank drew $23.5 billion of its swap line; the balance was repaid after three days. The other central banks did not draw on their lines. The temporary arrangements lapsed after thirty days.

Table 4.1

Federal Reserve standing reciprocal currency arrangements, June 30, 2004

Millions of U.S. dollars

Institution	Amount of facility	Amount drawn
Bank of Canada	2,000	0
Bank of Mexico	3,000	0
Temporary reciprocal currency arrangements of September 2001		
European Central Bank	50,000	23,500*
Bank of England	30,000	0
Bank of Canada	10,000†	0

* Total drawings on September 12, 13, and 14, 2001. Balance repaid as of September 15, 2001.

† Includes 2,000 from existing arrangement (see upper panel).

International Banking

The Federal Reserve is interested in the international activities of banks, not only because it functions as a bank supervisor but also because such activities are often close substitutes for domestic banking activities and need to be monitored carefully to help interpret U.S. monetary and credit conditions. Moreover, international banking institutions are important vehicles for capital flows into and out of the United States.

Where international banking activities are conducted depends on such factors as the business needs of customers, the scope of operations permitted by a country's legal and regulatory framework, and tax considerations. The international activities of U.S.-chartered banks include lending to and accepting deposits from foreign customers at the banks' U.S. offices and engaging in other financial transactions with foreign counterparts. However, the bulk of the international business of U.S.-chartered banks takes place at their branch offices located abroad and at their foreign-incorporated subsidiaries, usually wholly owned. Much of the activity of foreign branches and subsidiaries of U.S. banks has been Eurocurrency[1] business—that is, taking deposits and lending in currencies other than that of the country in which the banking office is located. Increasingly, U.S. banks are also offering a range of sophisticated financial products to residents of other countries and to U.S. firms abroad.

The international role of U.S. banks has a counterpart in foreign bank operations in the United States. U.S. offices of foreign banks actively participate as both borrowers and investors in U.S. domestic money markets and are active in the market for loans to U.S. businesses. (See chapter 5 for a discussion of the Federal Reserve's supervision and regulation of the international activities of U.S. banks and the U.S. activities of foreign banks.)

International banking by both U.S.-based and foreign banks facilitates the holding of Eurodollar deposits—dollar deposits in banking offices outside the United States—by nonbank U.S. entities. Similarly, Eurodollar loans—dollar loans from banking offices outside the United States—can be an important source of credit for U.S. companies (banks and nonbanks). Because they are close substitutes for deposits at domestic banks, Eurodollar deposits of nonbank U.S. entities at foreign branches of U.S. banks are included in the U.S. monetary aggregate M3; Eurodollar deposits of nonbank U.S. entities at all other banking offices in the United Kingdom and Canada are also included in M3. (See page 21 for a discussion of U.S. monetary aggregates.)

---

1. The term *Eurocurrency* should not be confused with *euro*, the common currency of several European Union countries.

The Federal Reserve has supervisory and regulatory authority over a wide range of financial institutions and activities. It works with other federal and state supervisory authorities to ensure the safety and soundness of financial institutions, stability in the financial markets, and fair and equitable treatment of consumers in their financial transactions. As the U.S. central bank, the Federal Reserve also has extensive and well-established relationships with the central banks and financial supervisors of other countries, which enables it to coordinate its actions with those of other countries when managing international financial crises and supervising institutions with a substantial international presence.

The Federal Reserve has responsibility for supervising and regulating the following segments of the banking industry to ensure safe and sound banking practices and compliance with banking laws:

- bank holding companies, including diversified financial holding companies formed under the Gramm-Leach-Bliley Act of 1999 and foreign banks with U.S. operations
- state-chartered banks that are members of the Federal Reserve System (state member banks)
- foreign branches of member banks
- Edge and agreement corporations, through which U.S. banking organizations may conduct international banking activities
- U.S. state-licensed branches, agencies, and representative offices of foreign banks
- nonbanking activities of foreign banks

Although the terms *bank supervision* and *bank regulation* are often used interchangeably, they actually refer to distinct, but complementary, activities. Bank supervision involves the monitoring, inspecting, and examining of banking organizations to assess their condition and their compliance with relevant laws and regulations. When a banking organization within the Federal Reserve's supervisory jurisdiction is found to be noncompliant or to have other problems, the Federal Reserve may use its supervisory authority to take formal or informal action to have the organization correct the problems.

Bank regulation entails issuing specific regulations and guidelines governing the operations, activities, and acquisitions of banking organizations.

Responsibilities of the Federal Banking Agencies

The primary supervisor of a domestic banking institution is generally determined by the type of institution that it is and the governmental authority that granted it permission to commence business.

The Federal Reserve shares supervisory and regulatory responsibilities for domestic banking institutions with the Office of the Comptroller of the Currency (OCC), the Federal Deposit Insurance Corporation (FDIC), and the Office of Thrift Supervision (OTS) at the federal level, and with the banking departments of the various states. The primary supervisor of a domestic banking institution is generally determined by the type of institution that it is and the governmental authority that granted it permission to commence business (commonly referred to as a charter). Banks that are chartered by a state government are referred to as state banks; banks that are chartered by the OCC, which is a bureau of the Department of the Treasury, are referred to as national banks.

The Federal Reserve has primary supervisory authority for state banks that elect to become members of the Federal Reserve System (state member banks). State banks that are not members of the Federal Reserve System (state nonmember banks) are supervised by the FDIC. In addition to being supervised by the Federal Reserve or FDIC, all state banks are supervised by their chartering state. The OCC supervises national banks. All national banks must become members of the Federal Reserve System. This dual federal–state banking system has evolved partly out of the complexity of the U.S. financial system, with its many kinds of depository institutions and numerous chartering authorities. It has also resulted from a wide variety of federal and state laws and regulations designed to remedy problems that the U.S. commercial banking system has faced over its history.

Banks are often owned or controlled by another company. These companies are referred to as bank holding companies. The Federal Reserve has supervisory authority for all bank holding companies, regardless of whether the subsidiary bank of the holding company is a national bank, state member bank, or state nonmember bank.

Savings associations, another type of depository institution, have historically focused on residential mortgage lending. The OTS, which is a bureau of the Department of the Treasury, charters and supervises federal savings associations and also supervises companies that own or control a savings association. These companies are referred to as thrift holding companies.

The FDIC insures the deposits of banks and savings associations up to certain limits established by law. As the insurer, the FDIC has special examination authority to determine the condition of an insured bank or savings association for insurance purposes.

Table 5.1 summarizes the supervisory responsibilities of the Federal Reserve and other federal banking agencies.

Table 5.1

Federal supervisor and regulator of corporate components of banking organizations in the United States

Component	Supervisor and regulator
Bank holding companies (including financial holding companies)	FR
Nonbank subsidiaries of bank holding companies	FR/Functional regulator[1]
National banks	OCC
State banks Members Nonmembers	FR FDIC
Thrift holding companies	OTS
Savings banks	OTS/FDIC/FR
Savings and loan associations	OTS
Edge and agreement corporations	FR
Foreign banks[2] Branches and agencies[3] State-licensed Federally licensed Representative offices	FR/FDIC OCC/FR/FDIC FR

NOTE: FR = Federal Reserve; OCC = Office of the Comptroller of the Currency; FDIC = Federal Deposit Insurance Corporation; OTS = Office of Thrift Supervision

1. Nonbank subsidiaries engaged in securities, commodities, or insurance activities are supervised and regulated by their appropriate functional regulators. Such functionally regulated subsidiaries include a broker, dealer, investment adviser, and investment company registered with and regulated by the Securities and Exchange Commission (or, in the case of an investment adviser, registered with any state); an insurance company or insurance agent subject to supervision by a state insurance regulator; and a subsidiary engaged in commodity activities regulated by the Commodity Futures Trading Commission.

2. Applies to direct operations in the United States. Foreign banks may also have indirect operations in the United States through their ownership of U.S. banking organizations.

3. The FDIC has responsibility for branches that are insured.

Federal Financial Institutions Examination Council

To promote consistency in the examination and supervision of banking organizations, in 1978 Congress created the Federal Financial Institutions Examination Council (FFIEC). The FFIEC is composed of the chairpersons of the FDIC and the National Credit Union Administration, the comptroller of the currency, the director of the OTS, and a governor of the Federal Reserve Board appointed by the Board Chairman. The FFIEC's purposes are to prescribe uniform federal principles and standards for the examination of depository institutions, to promote coordination of bank supervision among the federal agencies that regulate financial institutions, and to encourage better coordination of federal and state regulatory activities. Through the FFIEC, state and federal regulatory agencies may exchange views on important regulatory issues. Among other things, the FFIEC has developed uniform financial reports for federally supervised banks to file with their federal regulator.

The main objective of the supervisory process is to evaluate the overall safety and soundness of the banking organization.

Supervisory Process

The main objective of the supervisory process is to evaluate the overall safety and soundness of the banking organization. This evaluation includes an assessment of the organization's risk-management systems, financial condition, and compliance with applicable banking laws and regulations.

The supervisory process entails both on-site examinations and inspections and off-site surveillance and monitoring. Typically, state member banks must have an on-site examination at least once every twelve months. Banks that have assets of less than $250 million and that meet certain management, capital, and other criteria may be examined once every eighteen months. The Federal Reserve coordinates its examinations with those of the bank's chartering state and may alternate exam cycles with the bank's state supervisor.

The Federal Reserve generally conducts an annual inspection of large bank holding companies (companies with consolidated assets of $1 billion or greater) and smaller bank holding companies that have significant non-bank assets. Small, noncomplex bank holding companies are subject to a special supervisory program that permits a more flexible approach that relies on off-site monitoring and the supervisory ratings of the lead subsidiary depository institution. When evaluating the consolidated condition of the holding company, Federal Reserve examiners rely heavily on the results of the examination of the company's subsidiary banks by the primary federal or state banking authority, to minimize duplication of efforts and reduce burden on the banking organization.

Risk-Focused Supervision

With the largest banking organizations growing in both size and complexity, the Federal Reserve has moved towards a risk-focused approach to supervision that is more a continuous process than a point-in-time examination. The goal of the risk-focused supervision process is to identify the greatest risks to a banking organization and assess the ability of the organization's management to identify, measure, monitor, and control these risks. Under the risk-focused approach, Federal Reserve examiners focus on those business activities that may pose the greatest risk to the organization.

Supervisory Rating System

The results of an on-site examination or inspection are reported to the board of directors and management of the bank or holding company in a report of examination or inspection, which includes a confidential supervisory rating of the financial condition of the bank or holding company. The supervisory rating system is a supervisory tool that all of the federal and state banking agencies use to communicate to banking organizations the agency's assessment of the organization and to identify institutions that raise concern or require special attention. This rating system for banks is commonly referred to as CAMELS, which is an acronym for the six components of the rating system: capital adequacy, asset quality, management and administration, earnings, liquidity, and sensitivity to market risk. The Federal Reserve also uses a supervisory rating system for bank holding companies, referred to as RFI/C(D), that takes into account risk management, financial condition, potential impact of the parent company and nondepository subsidiaries on the affiliated depository institutions, and the CAMELS rating of the affiliated depository institutions.[1]

Financial Regulatory Reports

In carrying out their supervisory activities, Federal Reserve examiners and supervisory staff rely on many sources of financial and other information about banking organizations, including reports of recent examinations and inspections, information published in the financial press and elsewhere, and the standard financial regulatory reports filed by institutions.

---

1. The risk-management component has four subcomponents that reflect the effectiveness of the banking organization's risk management and controls: board and senior management oversight; policies, procedures, and limits; risk monitoring and management information systems; and internal controls. The financial-condition component has four subcomponents reflecting an assessment of the quality of the banking organization's capital, assets, earnings, and liquidity.

The financial report for banks is the Consolidated Reports of Condition and Income, often referred to as the Call Report. It is used to prepare the Uniform Bank Performance Report, which employs ratio analysis to detect unusual or significant changes in a bank's financial condition that may warrant supervisory attention. The financial report for bank holding companies is the Consolidated Financial Statements for Bank Holding Companies (the FR Y-9 series).

The number and type of report forms that must be filed by a banking organization depend on the size of the organization, the scope of its operations, and the types of activities that it conducts either directly or through a subsidiary. The report forms filed by larger institutions that engage in a wider range of activities are generally more numerous and more detailed than those filed by smaller organizations.

Off-Site Monitoring

The Federal Reserve plays a significant role in promoting sound accounting policies and meaningful public disclosure by financial institutions.

In its ongoing off-site supervision of banks and bank holding companies, the Federal Reserve uses automated screening systems to identify organizations with poor or deteriorating financial profiles and to help detect adverse trends developing in the banking industry. The System to Estimate Examinations Ratings (SEER) statistically estimates an institution's supervisory rating based on prior examination data and information that banks provide in their quarterly Call Report filings. This information enables the Federal Reserve to better direct examiner resources to those institutions needing supervisory attention.

Accounting Policy and Disclosure

Enhanced market discipline is an important component of bank supervision. Accordingly, the Federal Reserve plays a significant role in promoting sound accounting policies and meaningful public disclosure by financial institutions. In 1991, Congress passed the Federal Deposit Insurance Corporation Improvement Act, emphasizing the importance of financial institution accounting, auditing, and control standards. In addition, the Sarbanes-Oxley Act of 2002 seeks to improve the accuracy and reliability of corporate disclosures and to detect and address corporate and accounting fraud. Through its supervision and regulation function, the Federal Reserve seeks to strengthen the accounting, audit, and control standards related to financial institutions. The Federal Reserve is involved in the development of international and domestic capital, accounting, financial disclosure, and other supervisory standards. Federal Reserve examiners also review the quality of financial institutions' disclosure practices. Public disclosure allows market participants to assess the strength of individual institutions and is a critical element in market discipline.

Umbrella Supervision and Coordination with Other Functional Regulators

In addition to owning banks, bank holding companies also may own broker-dealers engaged in securities activities or insurance companies. Indeed, one of the primary purposes of the Gramm-Leach-Bliley Act (GLB Act), enacted in 1999, was to allow banks, securities broker-dealers, and insurance companies to affiliate with each other through the bank holding company structure. To take advantage of the expanded affiliations permitted by the GLB Act, a bank holding company must meet certain capital, managerial, and other requirements and must elect to become a "financial holding company." When a bank holding company or financial holding company owns a subsidiary broker-dealer or insurance company, the Federal Reserve seeks to coordinate its supervisory responsibilities with those of the subsidiary's functional regulator—the Securities and Exchange Commission (SEC) in the case of a broker-dealer and the state insurance authorities in the case of an insurance company.

The Federal Reserve's role as the supervisor of a bank holding company or financial holding company is to review and assess the consolidated organization's operations, risk-management systems, and capital adequacy to ensure that the holding company and its nonbank subsidiaries do not threaten the viability of the company's depository institutions. In this role, the Federal Reserve serves as the "umbrella supervisor" of the consolidated organization. In fulfilling this role, the Federal Reserve relies to the fullest extent possible on information and analysis provided by the appropriate supervisory authority of the company's bank, securities, or insurance subsidiaries.

Anti-Money-Laundering Program

To enhance domestic security following the terrorist attacks of September 11, 2001, Congress passed the USA Patriot Act, which contained provisions for fighting international money laundering and for blocking terrorists' access to the U.S. financial system. The provisions of the act that affect banking organizations were generally set forth as amendments to the Bank Secrecy Act (BSA), which was enacted in 1970.

The BSA requires financial institutions doing business in the United States to report large currency transactions and to retain certain records, including information about persons involved in large currency transactions and about suspicious activity related to possible violations of federal law, such as money laundering, terrorist financing, and other financial crimes. The BSA also prohibits the use of foreign bank accounts to launder illicit funds or to avoid U.S. taxes and statutory restrictions.

The Department of the Treasury maintains primary responsibility for issuing and enforcing regulations to implement this statute. However, Treasury has delegated to the federal financial regulatory agencies responsibility for monitoring banks' compliance with the BSA. The Federal Reserve Board's Regulation H requires banking organizations to develop a written program for BSA compliance. During examinations of state member banks and U.S. branches and agencies of foreign banks, Federal Reserve examiners verify an institution's compliance with the recordkeeping and reporting requirements of the BSA and with related regulations, including those related to economic sanctions imposed by Congress against certain countries, as implemented by the Office of Foreign Assets Control.

Business Continuity

After September 11, 2001, the Federal Reserve implemented a number of measures to promote the continuous operation of financial markets and to ensure the continuity of Federal Reserve operations in the event of a future crisis. The process of strengthening the resilience of the private-sector financial system—focusing on organizations with systemic elements—is largely accomplished through the existing regulatory framework. In 2003, responding to the need for further guidance for financial institutions in this area, the Federal Reserve Board, the OCC, and the SEC issued the "Interagency Paper on Sound Practices to Strengthen the Resilience of the U.S. Financial System." The paper sets forth sound practices for the financial industry to ensure a rapid recovery of the U.S. financial system in the event of a wide-scale disruption that may include loss or inaccessibility of staff. Many of the concepts in the paper amplify long-standing and well-recognized principles relating to safeguarding information and the ability to recover and resume essential financial services.

Other Supervisory Activities

The Federal Reserve conducts on-site examinations of banks to ensure compliance with consumer protection laws (discussed in chapter 6) as well as compliance in other areas, such as fiduciary activities, transfer agency, securities clearing agency, government and municipal securities dealing, securities credit lending, and information technology. Further, in light of the importance of information technology to the safety and soundness of banking organizations, the Federal Reserve has the authority to examine the operations of certain independent organizations that provide information technology services to supervised banking organizations.

Enforcement

If the Federal Reserve determines that a state member bank or bank holding company has problems that affect the institution's safety and soundness or is not in compliance with laws and regulations, it may take a supervisory action to ensure that the institution undertakes corrective measures. Typically, such findings are communicated to the management and directors of a banking organization in a written report. The management and directors are then asked to address all identified problems voluntarily and to take measures to ensure that the problems are corrected and will not recur. Most problems are resolved promptly after they are brought to the attention of an institution's management and directors. In some situations, however, the Federal Reserve may need to take an informal supervisory action, requesting that an institution adopt a board resolution or agree to the provisions of a memorandum of understanding to address the problem.

If necessary, the Federal Reserve may take formal enforcement actions to compel the management and directors of a troubled banking organization, or persons associated with it, to address the organization's problems. For example, if an institution has significant deficiencies or fails to comply with an informal action, the Federal Reserve may enter into a written agreement with the troubled institution or may issue a cease-and-desist order against the institution or against an individual associated with the institution, such as an officer or director. The Federal Reserve may also assess a fine, remove an officer or director from office and permanently bar him or her from the banking industry, or both. All final enforcement orders issued by the Board and all written agreements executed by Reserve Banks are available to the public on the Board's web site.

Supervision of International Operations of U.S. Banking Organizations

The Federal Reserve also has supervisory and regulatory responsibility for the international operations of member banks (that is, national and state member banks) and bank holding companies. These responsibilities include

- authorizing the establishment of foreign branches of national banks and state member banks and regulating the scope of their activities;
- chartering and regulating the activities of Edge and agreement corporations, which are specialized institutions used for international and foreign business;
- authorizing foreign investments of member banks, Edge and agreement corporations, and bank holding companies and regulating the activities of foreign firms acquired by such investors; and
- establishing supervisory policy and practices regarding foreign lending by state member banks.

Under federal law, U.S. banking organizations generally may conduct a wider range of activities abroad than they may conduct in this country.

Under federal law, U.S. banking organizations generally may conduct a wider range of activities abroad than they may conduct in this country.

The Board has broad discretionary powers to regulate the foreign activities of member banks and bank holding companies so that, in financing U.S. trade and investments abroad, U.S. banking organizations can be fully competitive with institutions of the host country. U.S. banks also may conduct deposit and loan business in U.S. markets outside their home states through Edge and agreement corporations if the operations of the corporations are related to international transactions.

The Federal Reserve examines the international operations of state member banks, Edge and agreement corporations, and bank holding companies principally at the U.S. head offices of these organizations. When appropriate, the Federal Reserve will conduct an examination at the foreign operations of a U.S. banking organization in order to review the accuracy of financial and operational information maintained at the head office as well as to test the organization's adherence to safe and sound banking practices and to evaluate its efforts to implement corrective measures. Examinations abroad are conducted in cooperation with the responsible foreign-country supervisor.

Supervision of U.S. Activities of Foreign Banking Organizations

Although foreign banks have been operating in the United States for more than a century, before 1978 the U.S. branches and agencies of these banks were not subject to supervision or regulation by any federal banking agency. When Congress enacted the International Banking Act of 1978 (IBA), it created a federal regulatory structure for the activities of foreign banks with U.S. branches and agencies. The IBA established a policy of "national treatment" for foreign banks operating in the United States to promote competitive equality between them and domestic institutions. This policy generally gives foreign banking organizations operating in the United States the same powers as U.S. banking organizations and subjects them to the same restrictions and obligations that apply to the domestic operations of U.S. banking organizations.

The Foreign Bank Supervision Enhancement Act of 1991 (FBSEA) increased the Federal Reserve's supervisory responsibility and authority over the U.S. operations of foreign banking organizations and eliminated gaps in the supervision and regulation of foreign banking organizations. The FBSEA amended the IBA to require foreign banks to obtain Federal Reserve approval before establishing branches, agencies, or commercial lending company subsidiaries in the United States. An application by a foreign bank to establish such offices or subsidiaries generally may be approved only if the Board determines that the foreign bank and any foreign-bank parents engage in banking business outside the United States and are subject to comprehensive supervision or regulation on a consolidated basis by their home-country supervisors. The Board may also take into account other factors, such as whether the home-country supervisor has consented to the proposed new office or subsidiary, the financial and managerial resources of the foreign bank, the condition of any existing U.S. offices, the bank's compliance with U.S. law, the extent of access by the Federal Reserve to information on the foreign bank from the bank and its home-country supervisor, and whether both the foreign bank and its home-country supervisor have taken actions to combat money laundering. The Board's prior approval is also required before a foreign bank may establish a representative office and, in approving the establishment of such an office, the Board takes the above-mentioned standards into account to the extent deemed appropriate.

The FBSEA also increased the responsibility and the authority of the Federal Reserve to regularly examine the U.S. operations of foreign banks. Under the FBSEA, all branches and agencies of foreign banks must be examined on-site at least once every twelve months, although this period may be extended to eighteen months if the branch or agency meets certain criteria. Supervisory actions resulting from examinations may be taken by the Federal Reserve alone or with other agencies. Representative offices are also subject to examination by the Federal Reserve.

The Federal Reserve coordinates the supervisory program for the U.S. operations of foreign banking organizations with the other federal and state banking agencies. Since a foreign banking organization may have both federally and state-chartered offices in the United States, the Federal Reserve plays a key role in assessing the condition of the organization's entire U.S. operations and the foreign banking organization's ability to support its U.S. operations. In carrying out their supervisory responsibilities, the Federal Reserve and other U.S. supervisors rely on two supervisory tools: SOSA rankings and ROCA ratings. SOSA (the Strength of Support Assessment) is the examiners' assessment of a foreign bank's ability to provide support for its U.S. operations. The ROCA rating is an assessment of the organization's U.S. activities in terms of its risk management, operational controls, compliance, and asset quality.

Under the Bank Holding Company Act and the IBA, the Federal Reserve is also responsible for approving, reviewing, and monitoring the U.S. nonbanking activities of foreign banking organizations that have a branch, agency, commercial lending company, or subsidiary bank in the United States. In addition, such foreign banks must obtain Federal Reserve approval to acquire more than 5 percent of the shares of a U.S. bank or bank holding company.

Supervision of Transactions with Affiliates

As part of the supervisory process, the Federal Reserve also evaluates transactions between a bank and its affiliates to determine the effect of the transactions on the bank's condition and to ascertain whether the transac-

The Federal Reserve evaluates transactions between a bank and its affiliates to determine the effect of the transactions on the bank's condition.

tions are consistent with sections 23A and 23B of the Federal Reserve Act, as implemented by the Federal Reserve Board's Regulation W. Since the GLB Act increased the range of affiliations permitted to banking organizations, sections 23A and 23B play an increasingly important role in limiting the risk to depository institutions from these broader affiliations. Among other things, section 23A prohibits a bank from purchasing an affiliate's low-quality assets. In addition, it limits a bank's loans and other extensions of credit to any single affiliate to 10 percent of the bank's capital and surplus, and it limits loans and other extensions of credit to all affiliates in the aggregate to 20 percent of the bank's capital and surplus. Section 23B requires that all transactions between a bank and its affiliates be on terms that are substantially the same, or at least as favorable, as those prevailing at the time for comparable transactions with nonaffiliated companies. The Federal Reserve Board is the only banking agency that has the authority to exempt any bank from these requirements. During the course of an examination, examiners review a banking organization's intercompany transactions for compliance with these statutes and Regulation W.

The Federal Reserve establishes standards designed to ensure that banking organizations operate in a safe and sound manner and in accordance with applicable law.

Regulatory Functions

As a bank regulator, the Federal Reserve establishes standards designed to ensure that banking organizations operate in a safe and sound manner and in accordance with applicable law. These standards may take the form of regulations, rules, policy guidelines, or supervisory interpretations and may be established under specific provisions of a law or under more general legal authority. Regulatory standards may be either restrictive (limiting the scope of a banking organization's activities) or permissive (authorizing banking organizations to engage in certain activities). (For a complete list of Federal Reserve regulations, see appendix A.)

In many cases, the Federal Reserve Board's regulations are adopted to implement specific legislative initiatives or requirements passed by Congress. These statutory provisions may have been adopted by Congress to respond to past crises or problems or to update the nation's banking laws to respond to changes in the marketplace. For example, in response to the savings and loan crisis and financial difficulties in the banking industry in the late 1980s and early 1990s, Congress enacted several laws to improve the condition of individual institutions and of the overall banking industry, including the Competitive Equality Banking Act of 1987; the Financial Institutions Reform, Recovery, and Enforcement Act of 1989; and the Federal Deposit Insurance Corporation Improvement Act of 1991. These legislative initiatives restricted banking practices, limited supervisors' discretion in dealing with weak banks, imposed new regulatory requirements—including prompt corrective action—and strengthened supervisory oversight overall.

More recently, Congress has adopted other laws to respond to the growing integration of banking markets, both geographically and functionally, and the increasing convergence of banking, securities, and insurance activities. The Riegle-Neal Interstate Banking and Branching Efficiency Act of 1994 significantly reduced the legal barriers that had restricted the ability of banks and bank holding companies to expand their activities across state lines. In 1999, Congress passed the GLB Act, which repealed certain Depression-era banking laws and permitted banks to affiliate with securities and insurance firms within financial holding companies.

Acquisitions and Mergers

Under the authority assigned to the Federal Reserve by the Bank Holding Company Act of 1956 as amended, the Bank Merger Act of 1960, and the Change in Bank Control Act of 1978, the Federal Reserve Board maintains broad authority over the structure of the banking system in the United States.

The Bank Holding Company Act assigned to the Federal Reserve primary responsibility for supervising and regulating the activities of bank holding companies. Through this act, Congress sought to achieve two basic objectives: (1) to avoid the creation of a monopoly or the restraint of trade in the banking industry through the acquisition of additional banks by bank holding companies and (2) to keep banking and commerce separate by restricting the nonbanking activities of bank holding companies. Historically, bank holding companies could engage only in banking activities and other activities that the Federal Reserve determined to be closely related to banking. But since the passage of the GLB Act, a bank holding company that qualifies to become a financial holding company may engage in a broader range of financially related activities, including full-scope securities underwriting and dealing, insurance underwriting and sales, and merchant banking. A bank holding company seeking financial holding company status must file a written declaration with the Federal Reserve System, certifying that the company meets the capital, managerial, and other requirements to be a financial holding company.

Bank Acquisitions

Under the Bank Holding Company Act, a firm that seeks to become a bank holding company must first obtain approval from the Federal Reserve. The act defines a *bank holding company* as any company that directly or indirectly owns, controls, or has the power to vote 25 percent or more of any class of the voting shares of a bank; controls in any manner the election of a majority of the directors or trustees of a bank; or is found to exercise a controlling influence over the management or policies of a bank. A bank holding company must obtain the approval of the Federal

Reserve before acquiring more than 5 percent of the shares of an additional bank or bank holding company. All bank holding companies must file certain reports with the Federal Reserve System.

When considering applications to acquire a bank or a bank holding company, the Federal Reserve is required to take into account the likely effects of the acquisition on competition, the convenience and needs of the communities to be served, the financial and managerial resources and future prospects of the companies and banks involved, and the effectiveness of the company's policies to combat money laundering. In the case of an interstate bank acquisition, the Federal Reserve also must consider certain other factors and may not approve the acquisition if the resulting organization would control more than 10 percent of all deposits held by insured depository institutions. When a foreign bank seeks to acquire a U.S. bank, the Federal Reserve also must consider whether the foreign banking organization is subject to comprehensive supervision or regulation on a consolidated basis by its home-country supervisor.

The Federal Reserve is responsible for changes in the control of bank holding companies and state member banks.

Bank Mergers

Another responsibility of the Federal Reserve is to act on proposed bank mergers when the resulting institution would be a state member bank. The Bank Merger Act of 1960 sets forth the factors to be considered in evaluating merger applications. These factors are similar to those that must be considered in reviewing bank acquisition proposals by bank holding companies. To ensure that all merger applications are evaluated in a uniform manner, the act requires that the responsible agency request reports from the Department of Justice and from the other approving banking agencies addressing the competitive impact of the transaction.

Other Changes in Bank Control

The Change in Bank Control Act of 1978 authorizes the federal bank regulatory agencies to deny proposals by a single "person" (which includes an individual or an entity), or several persons acting in concert, to acquire control of an insured bank or a bank holding company. The Federal Reserve is responsible for approving changes in the control of bank holding companies and state member banks, and the FDIC and the OCC are responsible for approving changes in the control of insured state nonmember and national banks, respectively. In considering a proposal under the act, the Federal Reserve must review several factors, including the financial condition, competence, experience, and integrity of the acquiring person or group of persons; the effect of the transaction on competition; and the adequacy of the information provided by the acquiring party.

Formation and Activities of Financial Holding Companies

As authorized by the GLB Act, the Federal Reserve Board's regulations allow a bank holding company or a foreign banking organization to become a financial holding company and engage in an expanded array of financial activities if the company meets certain capital, managerial, and other criteria. Permissible activities for financial holding companies include conducting securities underwriting and dealing, serving as an insurance agent and underwriter, and engaging in merchant banking. Other permissible activities include those that the Federal Reserve Board, after consulting with the Secretary of the Treasury, determines to be financial in nature or incidental to financial activities. Financial holding companies also may engage to a limited extent in a nonfinancial activity if the Board determines that the activity is complementary to one or more of the company's financial activities and would not pose a substantial risk to the safety or soundness of depository institutions or the financial system.

Capital Adequacy Standards

A key goal of banking regulation is to ensure that banks maintain sufficient capital to absorb reasonably likely losses. In 1989, the federal banking regulators adopted a common standard for measuring capital adequacy that is broadly based on the risks of an institution's investments. This common standard, in turn, was based on the 1988 agreement "International Convergence of Capital Measurement and Capital Standards" (commonly known as the Basel Accord) developed by the Basel Committee on Banking Supervision. This committee, which is associated with the Bank for International Settlements headquartered in Switzerland, is composed of representatives of the central banks or bank supervisory authorities from Belgium, Canada, France, Germany, Italy, Japan, Luxembourg, the Netherlands, Spain, Sweden, Switzerland, the United Kingdom, and the United States.

A key goal of banking regulation is to ensure that banks maintain sufficient capital to absorb reasonably likely losses.

The risk-based capital standards require institutions that assume greater risk to hold higher levels of capital. Moreover, these standards take into account risks associated with activities that are not included on a bank's balance sheet, such as the risks arising from commitments to make loans. Because they have been accepted by the bank supervisory authorities of most of the countries with major international banking centers, these standards promote safety and soundness and reduce competitive inequities among banking organizations operating within an increasingly global market.

Recognizing that the existing risk-based capital standards were in need of significant enhancements to address the activities of complex banking organizations, the Basel Committee began work to revise the Basel Accord in 1999 and, in June 2004, endorsed a revised framework, which is referred to as Basel II. Basel II has three "pillars" that make up the framework for assessing capital adequacy. Pillar I, minimum regulatory capital requirements, more closely aligns banking organizations' capital levels with their underlying risks. Pillar II, supervisory oversight, requires supervisors to evaluate banking organizations' capital adequacy and to encourage better risk-management techniques. Pillar III, market discipline, calls for enhanced public disclosure of banking organizations' risk exposures.

Financial Disclosures by State Member Banks

State member banks that issue securities registered under the Securities Exchange Act of 1934 must disclose certain information of interest to investors, including annual and quarterly financial reports and proxy statements. By statute, the Federal Reserve administers these requirements and has adopted financial disclosure regulations for state member banks that are substantially similar to the SEC's regulations for other public companies.

Securities Credit

The Securities Exchange Act of 1934 requires the Federal Reserve to regulate the extension of credit used in connection with the purchase of securities. Through its regulations, the Board establishes the minimum amount the buyer must put up when purchasing a security. This minimum amount is known as the margin requirement. In fulfilling its responsibility under the act, the Federal Reserve limits the amount of credit that may be provided by securities brokers and dealers (Regulation T) and the amount of securities credit extended by banks and other lenders (Regulation U). These regulations generally apply to credit-financed purchases of securities traded on securities exchanges and certain securities traded over the counter when the credit is collateralized by such securities. In addition, Regulation X prohibits borrowers who are subject to U.S. laws from obtaining such credit overseas on terms more favorable than could be obtained from a domestic lender.

In general, compliance with the Federal Reserve's margin regulations is enforced by several federal regulatory agencies. The federal agencies that regulate financial institutions check for Regulation U compliance during examinations. The Federal Reserve checks for Regulation U compliance on the part of securities credit lenders not otherwise regulated by federal agencies. Compliance with Regulation T is verified during examinations of broker-dealers by the securities industry's self-regulatory organizations under the general oversight of the SEC.

The number of federal laws intended to protect consumers in credit and other financial transactions has been growing since the late 1960s. Congress has assigned to the Federal Reserve the duty of implementing many of these laws to ensure that consumers receive comprehensive information and fair treatment.

Among the Federal Reserve's responsibilities in this area are

- writing and interpreting regulations to carry out many of the major consumer protection laws,
- reviewing bank compliance with the regulations,
- investigating complaints from the public about state member banks' compliance with consumer protection laws,
- addressing issues of state and federal jurisdiction,
- testifying before Congress on consumer protection issues, and
- conducting community development activities.

In carrying out these responsibilities, the Federal Reserve is advised by its Consumer Advisory Council, whose members represent the interests of consumers, community groups, and creditors nationwide. Meetings of the council, which take place three times a year at the Federal Reserve Board in Washington, D.C., are open to the public.

Consumer Protection

Most financial transactions involving consumers are covered by consumer protection laws. These include transactions involving credit, charge, and debit cards issued by financial institutions and credit cards issued by retail establishments; automated teller machine transactions and other electronic fund transfers; deposit account transactions; automobile leases; mortgages and home equity loans; and lines of credit and other unsecured credit.

Writing and Interpreting Regulations

The Federal Reserve Board writes regulations to implement many of the major consumer protection laws. These regulations may cover not only banks but also certain businesses, including finance companies, mortgage brokers, retailers, and automobile dealers. For example, Congress passed the Truth in Lending Act to ensure that consumers have adequate information about credit. The Board implemented that law by writing Regulation Z, which requires banks and other creditors to provide detailed information to consumers about the terms and cost of consumer credit for mortgages, car loans, credit and charge cards, and other credit products. The Board also revises and updates its regulations to address new products or changes in technology, to implement changes to existing legislation, or to address problems encountered by consumers.

Educating Consumers about Consumer Protection Laws

Well-educated consumers are the best consumer protection in the market.

Well-educated consumers are the best consumer protection in the market. They know their rights and responsibilities, and they use the information provided in disclosures to shop and compare. The Federal Reserve Board maintains a consumer information web site with educational materials related to the consumer protection regulations developed by the Board (www.federalreserve.gov/consumers.htm). In addition, the Federal Reserve staff uses consumer surveys and focus groups to learn more about what issues are important to consumers and to develop and test additional educational resources.

Enforcing Consumer Protection Laws

The Federal Reserve has a comprehensive program to examine financial institutions and other entities that it supervises to ensure compliance with consumer protection laws and regulations. Its enforcement responsibilities generally extend only to state-chartered banks that are members of the Federal Reserve System and to certain foreign banking organizations. Other federal regulators are responsible for examining banks, thrift institutions, and credit unions under their jurisdictions and for taking enforcement action.

Each Reserve Bank has specially trained examiners who regularly evaluate banks' compliance with consumer protection laws and their Community Reinvestment Act (CRA) performance. Most banks are evaluated every forty-eight months, although large banks are examined every twenty-four months and poorly rated banks are examined more frequently.

To make the most effective and efficient use of resources while ensuring compliance with consumer protection laws and regulations, the Federal Reserve uses a risk-focused approach to supervision, focusing most intensely on those areas involving the greatest compliance risk. Examinations always include a comprehensive assessment of an institution's CRA performance in order to present to the public a full and fair portrait of the institution's efforts. Examiners also assess the broad range of large complex banking organizations' activities to determine the level and trend of compliance risk in the area of consumer protection.

In accordance with the Community Reinvestment Act of 1977, the Federal Reserve reviews a bank's efforts to meet the credit and community development needs of its entire community, including low- and moderate-income neighborhoods; for example, it looks at the extent to which a bank has programs that contribute to the building of affordable housing and to other aspects of community development. When deciding whether to approve an application for a bank acquisition or merger or for the formation of a bank holding company, the Federal Reserve takes into account an institution's performance under the CRA. An important aspect of the process is that it gives the public the opportunity to submit written comments on the proposal. These comments, which often provide insight into a financial institution's CRA performance, are reviewed by Federal Reserve staff and considered by the Board when it evaluates an application.

At the end of this chapter is a list of the consumer protection laws for which the Federal Reserve has rule-writing or enforcement responsibility, the dates the laws were enacted, and the highlights of the laws' provisions.

The Federal Reserve reviews a bank's efforts to meet the credit and community development needs of its entire community.

Consumer Complaint Program

The Federal Reserve responds to inquiries and complaints from the public about the policies and practices of financial institutions involving consumer protection issues. Each Reserve Bank has staff whose primary responsibility is to investigate consumer complaints about state member banks and refer complaints about other institutions to the appropriate regulatory agencies. The Federal Reserve's responses not only address the concerns raised but also educate consumers about financial matters.

The Federal Reserve Board maintains information on consumer inquiries and complaints in a database, which it regularly reviews to identify potential problems at individual financial institutions and, as required by the Federal Trade Commission Improvement Act, to uncover potentially unfair or deceptive practices within the banking industry. Complaint data are a critical component of the risk-focused supervisory program and are used as a risk factor to assess a bank's compliance with consumer regulations. Data about consumer complaints are also used to determine the need for future regulations or educational efforts.

Community Affairs

Community affairs programs at the Board and the twelve Federal Reserve Banks promote community development and fair and impartial access to credit. Community affairs offices at the Board and Reserve Banks engage in a wide variety of activities to help financial institutions, community-based organizations, government entities, and the public understand and address financial services issues that affect low- and moderate-income people and geographic regions. Each office responds to local needs in its District and establishes its own programs to

- foster depository institutions' active engagement in providing credit and other banking services to their entire communities, particularly traditionally underserved markets;
- encourage mutually beneficial cooperation among community organizations, government agencies, financial institutions, and other community development practitioners;
- develop greater public awareness of the benefits and risks of financial products and of the rights and responsibilities that derive from community investment and fair lending regulations; and
- promote among policy makers, community leaders, and private-sector decision makers a better understanding of the practices, processes, and resources that result in successful community development programs.

Each Federal Reserve Bank develops specific products and services to meet the informational needs of its region. The community affairs offices issue a wide array of publications, sponsor a variety of public forums, and provide technical information on community and economic development and on fair and equal access to credit and other banking services.

Consumer Protection Laws

The Fair Housing Act prohibits discrimination in the extension of housing credit.

- ***Fair Housing Act (1968)***
  Prohibits discrimination in the extension of housing credit on the basis of race, color, religion, national origin, sex, handicap, or family status.
- ***Truth in Lending Act (1968)***
  Requires uniform methods for computing the cost of credit and for disclosing credit terms. Gives borrowers the right to cancel, within three days, certain loans secured by their residences. Prohibits the unsolicited issuance of credit cards and limits cardholder liability for unauthorized use. Also imposes limitations on home equity loans with rates or fees above a specified threshold.
- ***Fair Credit Reporting Act (1970)***
  Protects consumers against inaccurate or misleading information in credit files maintained by credit-reporting agencies; requires credit-reporting agencies to allow credit applicants to correct erroneous reports.
- ***Flood Disaster Protection Act of 1973***
  Requires flood insurance on property in a flood hazard area that comes under the National Flood Insurance Program.
- ***Fair Credit Billing Act (1974)***
  Specifies how creditors must respond to billing-error complaints from consumers; imposes requirements to ensure that creditors handle ac-

counts fairly and promptly. Applies primarily to credit and charge card accounts (for example, store card and bank card accounts). Amended the Truth in Lending Act.

- *Equal Credit Opportunity Act (1974)*
  Prohibits discrimination in credit transactions on several bases, including sex, marital status, age, race, religion, color, national origin, the receipt of public assistance funds, or the exercise of any right under the Consumer Credit Protection Act. Requires creditors to grant credit to qualified individuals without requiring cosignature by spouses, to inform unsuccessful applicants in writing of the reasons credit was denied, and to allow married individuals to have credit histories on jointly held accounts maintained in the names of both spouses. Also entitles a borrower to a copy of a real estate appraisal report.

- *Real Estate Settlement Procedures Act of 1974*
  Requires that the nature and costs of real estate settlements be disclosed to borrowers. Also protects borrowers against abusive practices, such as kickbacks, and limits the use of escrow accounts.

- *Home Mortgage Disclosure Act of 1975*
  Requires mortgage lenders to annually disclose to the public data about the geographic distribution of their applications, originations, and purchases of home-purchase and home-improvement loans and refinancings. Requires lenders to report data on the ethnicity, race, sex, income of applicants and borrowers, and other data. Also directs the Federal Financial Institutions Examination Council, of which the Federal Reserve is a member, to make summaries of the data available to the public.

- *Consumer Leasing Act of 1976*
  Requires that institutions disclose the cost and terms of consumer leases, such as automobile leases.

- *Fair Debt Collection Practices Act (1977)*
  Prohibits abusive debt collection practices. Applies to banks that function as debt collectors for other entities.

- *Community Reinvestment Act of 1977*
  Encourages financial institutions to help meet the credit needs of their entire communities, particularly low- and moderate-income neighborhoods.

- *Right to Financial Privacy Act of 1978*
  Protects bank customers from the unlawful scrutiny of their financial records by federal agencies and specifies procedures that government authorities must follow when they seek information about a customer's financial records from a financial institution.

- *Electronic Fund Transfer Act (1978)*
  Establishes the basic rights, liabilities, and responsibilities of consumers who use electronic fund transfer services and of financial institutions that offer these services. Covers transactions conducted at automated teller machines, at point-of-sale terminals in stores, and through tele-

The Community Reinvestment Act encourages financial institutions to help meet the credit needs of their entire communities.

phone bill-payment plans and preauthorized transfers to and from a customer's account, such as direct deposit of salary or Social Security payments.

- *Federal Trade Commission Improvement Act (1980)*
  Authorizes the Federal Reserve to identify unfair or deceptive acts or practices by banks and to issue regulations to prohibit them. Using this authority, the Federal Reserve has adopted rules substantially similar to those adopted by the FTC that restrict certain practices in the collection of delinquent consumer debt, for example, practices related to late charges, responsibilities of cosigners, and wage assignments.
- *Expedited Funds Availability Act (1987)*
  Specifies when depository institutions must make funds deposited by check available to depositors for withdrawal. Requires institutions to disclose to customers their policies on funds availability.
- *Women's Business Ownership Act of 1988*
  Extends to applicants for business credit certain protections afforded consumer credit applicants, such as the right to an explanation for credit denial. Amended the Equal Credit Opportunity Act.
- *Fair Credit and Charge Card Disclosure Act of 1988*
  Requires that applications for credit cards that are sent through the mail, solicited by telephone, or made available to the public (for example, at counters in retail stores or through catalogs) contain information about key terms of the account. Amended the Truth in Lending Act.
- *Home Equity Loan Consumer Protection Act of 1988*
  Requires creditors to provide consumers with detailed information about open-end credit plans secured by the consumer's dwelling. Also regulates advertising of home equity loans and restricts the terms of home equity loan plans.
- *Truth in Savings Act (1991)*
  Requires that depository institutions disclose to depositors certain information about their accounts—including the annual percentage yield, which must be calculated in a uniform manner—and prohibits certain methods of calculating interest. Regulates advertising of savings accounts.
- *Home Ownership and Equity Protection Act of 1994*
  Provides additional disclosure requirements and substantive limitations on home-equity loans with rates or fees above a certain percentage or amount. Amended the Truth in Lending Act.
- *Gramm-Leach-Bliley Act, title V, subpart A, Disclosure of Nonpublic Personal Information (1999)*
  Describes the conditions under which a financial institution may disclose nonpublic personal information about consumers to nonaffiliated third parties, provides a method for consumers to opt out of information sharing with nonaffiliated third parties, and requires a financial institution to notify consumers about its privacy policies and practices.

The Fair Credit and Charge Card Disclosure Act requires that applications for credit cards contain information about key terms of the account.

- ***Fair and Accurate Credit Transaction Act of 2003***
  Enhances consumers' ability to combat identity theft, increases the accuracy of consumer reports, allows consumers to exercise greater control over the type and amount of marketing solicitations they receive, restricts the use and disclosure of sensitive medical information, and establishes uniform national standards in the regulation of consumer reporting. Amended the Fair Credit Reporting Act.

The Federal Reserve plays an important role in the U.S. payments system. The twelve Federal Reserve Banks provide banking services to depository institutions and to the federal government. For depository institutions, they maintain accounts and provide various payment services, including collecting checks, electronically transferring funds, and distributing and receiving currency and coin. For the federal government, the Reserve Banks act as fiscal agents, paying Treasury checks; processing electronic payments; and issuing, transferring, and redeeming U.S. government securities.

By creating the Federal Reserve System, Congress intended to eliminate the severe financial crises that had periodically swept the nation, especially the sort of financial panic that occurred in 1907. During that episode, payments were disrupted throughout the country because many banks and clearinghouses refused to clear checks drawn on certain other banks, a practice that contributed to the failure of otherwise solvent banks. To address these problems, Congress gave the Federal Reserve System the authority to establish a nationwide check-clearing system. The System, then, was to provide not only an elastic currency—that is, a currency that would expand or shrink in amount as economic conditions warranted— but also an efficient and equitable check-collection system.

Bank panic of 1907

Congress was also concerned about some banks' paying less than the full amount of checks deposited by their customers because some paying banks charged fees to presenting banks to pay checks. To avoid paying presentment fees, many collecting banks routed checks through banks that were not charged presentment fees by paying banks. This practice, called circuitous routing, resulted in extensive delays and inefficiencies in the check-collection system. In 1917, Congress amended the Federal Reserve Act to prohibit banks from charging the Reserve Banks presentment fees and to authorize nonmember banks as well as member banks to collect checks through the Federal Reserve System.

In passing the Monetary Control Act of 1980, Congress reaffirmed its intention that the Federal Reserve should promote an efficient nationwide payments system. The act subjects all depository institutions, not just member commercial banks, to reserve requirements and grants them equal access to Reserve Bank payment services. It also encourages competition between the Reserve Banks and private-sector providers of payment services by requiring the Reserve Banks to charge fees for certain payments services listed in the act and to recover the costs of providing these services over the long run.

The Federal Reserve performs an important role as an intermediary in clearing and settling interbank payments.

More recent congressional action has focused increasingly on improving the efficiency of the payments system by encouraging increased use of technology. In 1987, Congress enacted the Expedited Funds Availability Act (EFAA), which gave the Board, for the first time, the authority to regulate the payments system in general, not just those payments made through the Reserve Banks. The Board used its authority under the EFAA to revamp the check-return system, improve the presentment rights of private-sector banks, and establish rules governing the time that banks can hold funds from checks deposited into customer accounts before making the funds available for withdrawal. In 2003, Congress enacted the Check Clearing for the 21st Century Act, which further enhanced the efficiency of the payments system by reducing legal and practical impediments to check truncation and the electronic collection of checks, services that speed up check collection and reduce associated costs.

Financial Services

The U.S. payments system is the largest in the world. Each day, millions of transactions, valued in the trillions of dollars, are conducted between sellers and purchasers of goods, services, or financial assets. Most of the payments underlying those transactions flow between depository institutions, a large number of which maintain accounts with the Reserve Banks. The Federal Reserve therefore performs an important role as an intermediary in clearing and settling interbank payments. The Reserve

Banks settle payment transactions efficiently by debiting the accounts of the depository institutions making payments and by crediting the accounts of depository institutions receiving payments. Moreover, as the U.S. central bank, the Federal Reserve is immune from liquidity problems—not having sufficient funds to complete payment transactions—and credit problems that could disrupt its clearing and settlement activities.

The Federal Reserve plays a vital role in both the nation's retail and wholesale payments systems, providing a variety of financial services to depository institutions. Retail payments are generally for relatively small-dollar amounts and often involve a depository institution's retail clients—individuals and smaller businesses. The Reserve Banks' retail services include distributing currency and coin, collecting checks, and electronically transferring funds through the automated clearinghouse system. By contrast, wholesale payments are generally for large-dollar amounts and often involve a depository institution's large corporate customers or counterparties, including other financial institutions. The Reserve Banks' wholesale services include electronically transferring funds through the Fedwire Funds Service and transferring securities issued by the U.S. government, its agencies, and certain other entities through the Fedwire Securities Service. Because of the large amounts of funds that move through the Reserve Banks every day, the System has policies and procedures to limit the risk to the Reserve Banks from a depository institution's failure to make or settle its payments.

An important function of the Federal Reserve is ensuring that enough cash is in circulation to meet the public's demand.

Retail Services

Currency and Coin

An important function of the Federal Reserve is ensuring that enough cash—that is, currency and coin—is in circulation to meet the public's demand. When Congress established the Federal Reserve, it recognized that the public's demand for cash is variable. This demand increases or decreases seasonally and as the level of economic activity changes. For example, in the weeks leading up to a holiday season, depository institutions increase their orders of currency and coin from Reserve Banks to meet their customers' demand. Following the holiday season, depository institutions ship excess currency and coin back to the Reserve Banks, where it is credited to their accounts.

Each of the twelve Reserve Banks is authorized by the Federal Reserve Act to issue currency, and the Department of Treasury is authorized to issue coin. The Secretary of the Treasury approves currency designs, and the Treasury's Bureau of Engraving and Printing prints the notes. The Federal Reserve Board places an annual printing order with the bureau and pays the bureau for the cost of printing. The Federal Reserve Board coordinates shipments of currency to the Reserve Banks around the country. The Reserve Banks, in turn, issue the notes to the public through depository institutions. Federal Reserve notes are obligations of the Reserve Banks. The Reserve Banks secure the currency they issue with legally authorized collateral, most of which is in the form of U.S. Treasury securities held by the Reserve Banks. Coin, unlike currency, is issued by the Treasury, not the Reserve Banks. The Reserve Banks order coin from the Treasury's Bureau of the Mint and pay the Mint the full face value of coin, rather than the cost to produce it. The Reserve Banks then distribute coin to the public through depository institutions.

Demand Treasury note, 1861

Silver certificate, 1880

Although the issuance of paper money in this country dates back to 1690, the U.S. government did not issue paper currency with the intent that it circulate as money until 1861, when Congress approved the issuance of demand Treasury notes. All currency issued by the U.S. government since then remains legal tender, including silver certificates, which have a blue seal for the Department of the Treasury; United States notes, which have a red seal; and national bank notes, which have a brown seal. Today, nearly all currency in circulation is in the form of Federal Reserve notes, which were first issued in 1914 and have a green Treasury seal. Currency is redesigned periodically to incorporate new anti-counterfeiting features. When currency is redesigned, all previous Federal Reserve notes remain valid.

National bank note, Winters National Bank of Dayton, Ohio, 1901

When currency flows back to the Reserve Banks, each deposit is counted, verified, and authenticated. Notes that are too worn for recirculation (unfit notes) and those that are suspected of being counterfeit are culled out. Suspect notes are forwarded to the United States Secret Service, and unfit notes are destroyed at the Reserve Banks on behalf of the Treasury. Notes that can be recirculated to the public are held in Reserve Bank vaults, along with new notes, until they are needed to meet demand. Coin that is received by Reserve Banks is verified by weight rather than piece-counted, as currency is.

Today, currency and coin are used primarily for small–dollar transactions and thus account for only a small proportion of the total dollar value of all monetary transactions. During 2003, Reserve Banks delivered to depository institutions about 36.6 billion notes having a value of $633.4 billion and received from depository institutions about 35.7 billion notes having a value of $596.9 billion. Of the total received by Reserve Banks, 7.4 billion notes, with a face value of $101.3 billion, were deemed to be unfit to continue to circulate and were destroyed. The difference between the amount of currency paid to depository institutions and the amount of currency received from circulation equals the change in demand for currency resulting from economic activity. In 2003, the increase in demand was $36.5 billion.

Over the past five decades, the value of currency and coin in circulation has risen dramatically—from $31.2 billion in 1955 to $724.2 billion in 2003 (table 7.1).[1] The total number of notes in circulation (24.8 billion at

---

1. Current data on currency and coin can be found on the Board's web site (www.federalreserve.gov), under "Payment Systems."

the end of 2003) and the demand for larger denominations ($20, $50, and $100 notes) has also increased (table 7.2). In 1960, these larger denominations accounted for 64 percent of the total value of currency in circulation; by the end of 2003, they accounted for 95 percent. Because the U.S. dollar is highly regarded throughout the world as a stable and readily negotiable currency, much of the increased demand for larger-denomination notes has arisen outside of the United States. Although the exact value of U.S. currency held outside the country is unknown, Federal Reserve economists estimate that from one-half to two-thirds of all U.S. currency circulates abroad.

Table 7.1

Value of currency and coin in circulation, selected years, 1955–2003
Millions of dollars

Year	Currency*	Coin	Total
1955	29,242	1,916	31,158
1960	30,442	2,426	32,868
1965	38,029	4,027	42,056
1970	45,915	5,986	51,901
1975	68,059	8,285	76,344
1980	109,515	11,641	121,156
1985	182,003	15,456	197,459
1990	268,206	18,765	286,971
1995	401,517	22,727	424,244
2000	563,970	29,724	593,694
2001	612,273	31,028	643,301
2002	654,785	32,733	687,518
2003	690,267	33,927	724,194

* Currency in circulation includes Federal Reserve notes, silver certificates, United States notes, and national bank notes.

Table 7.2

Estimated value of currency in circulation by denomination, selected years, 1960–2003

Billions of dollars

Year	Denomination								Total
	1	2	5	10	20	50	100	Other*	
1960	1.5	.1	2.2	6.7	10.5	2.8	6.0	.6	30.4
1970	2.1	.1	2.9	8.4	16.6	4.4	10.9	.5	45.9
1980	3.1	.7	4.1	11.0	36.4	12.2	41.6	.4	109.5
1990	5.1	.8	6.3	12.6	69.0	33.9	140.2	.3	268.2
2000	7.7	1.2	8.9	14.5	98.6	55.1	377.7	.3	564.0
2003	8.2	1.4	9.7	15.2	107.8	59.9	487.8	.3	690.3

* Other denominations include the $500, $1,000, $5,000, and $10,000 notes. No denominations larger than $100 have been printed since 1946 or issued since 1969. The majority of these notes are held by private collectors, currency dealers, and financial institutions for display.

Check Processing

While cash is convenient for small-dollar transactions, for larger-value transactions individuals, businesses, and governments generally use checks or electronic funds transfers. Measured by the number used, checks continue to be the preferred noncash payment method; however, their use has begun to decline in favor of electronic methods. In 2001, the Federal Reserve conducted an extensive survey on the use of checks and other non-cash payment instruments in the United States and compared the results with a 1979 study of noncash payments and similar data collected in 1995. The survey results indicated that check usage peaked sometime during the mid-1990s and has declined since then. For example, the survey found that checks represented 59.5 percent of retail noncash payments in 2000, compared with 77.1 percent just five years earlier and 85.7 percent in 1979. The total value of checks paid declined from an estimated $50.7 trillion in 1979 to $39.3 trillion in 2000 (both in 2000 dollars).[2]

In 2004, the Federal Reserve conducted another study to determine the changes in noncash payments from 2000 to 2003. That study found that the number of noncash payments had grown since 2000 and that checks were the only payment instrument being used less frequently than in 2000

---

2. See Gerdes, Geoffrey R., and Jack K. Walton II, "The Use of Checks and Other Noncash Payment Instruments in the United States," *Federal Reserve Bulletin*, vol. 88 (August 2002), pp. 360–74.

(table 7.3). Chart 7.1 illustrates the changes in the distribution of noncash payments from 2000 to 2003.

Table 7.3
Number of noncash payments, 2000 and 2003

	2000 estimate (billions)	2003 estimate (billions)	CAGR*
Noncash payments	72.5	81.2	38%
Check	41.9	36.7	−4.3%
Credit card	15.6	19.0	6.7%
ACH	6.2	9.1	13.4%
Offline debit	5.3	10.3	24.9%
Online debit	3.0	5.3	21.0%
Electronic benefits transfers (EBTs)	0.5	0.8	15.4%

* Compound annual growth rate.

Chart 7.1
Distribution of number of noncash payments, 2000 and 2003

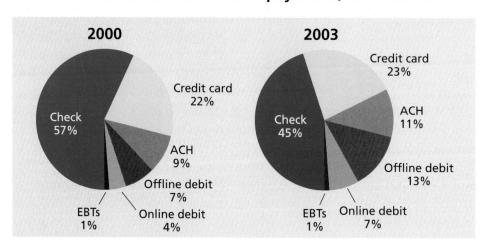

Of the estimated 36.7 billion checks paid in 2003, approximately 8.7 billion were "on-us checks," that is, checks deposited in the same institution on which they were drawn. In 2003, the Reserve Banks processed more than 58 percent of interbank checks, checks not drawn on the institution at which they were deposited. Depository institutions cleared the remaining checks through private arrangements among themselves. These private arrangements include sending checks directly to the depository institution on which they are drawn, depositing the checks for collection with a correspondent bank, or delivering the checks to a clearinghouse for exchange. Processing interbank checks requires a mechanism for exchanging the checks as well as for the related movement of funds, or settlement, among the depository institutions involved.

For checks collected through the Reserve Banks, the account of the collecting institution is credited for the value of the deposited checks in accordance with the availability schedules maintained by the Reserve Banks. These schedules reflect the time normally needed for the Reserve Banks to receive payments from the institutions on which the checks are drawn. Credit is usually given on the day of deposit or the next business day. In 2003, the Reserve Banks collected 16 billion checks with a value of $15.8 trillion (table 7.4).

Table 7.4
Number and value of checks collected by the Reserve Banks, selected years, 1920–2003

Number in millions; value in millions of dollars

Year	Number	Value
1920	424	149,784
1930	905	324,883
1940	1,184	280,436
1950	1,955	856,953
1960	3,419	1,154,121
1970	7,158	3,331,733
1980	15,716	8,038,026
1990	18,598	12,519,171
2000	16,994	13,849,084
2003	16,271	15,768,877

NOTE: In 2003, the Reserve Banks, acting as fiscal agents for the United States, also paid 267 million Treasury checks and 198 million postal money orders.

Since it was established, the Federal Reserve has worked with the private sector to improve the efficiency and cost-effectiveness of the check-collection system. Toward that end, the Federal Reserve and the banking industry developed bank routing numbers in the 1940s. These numbers are still printed on checks to identify the institution on which a check is drawn and to which the check must be presented for payment. In the 1950s, the magnetic ink character recognition (MICR) system for encoding pertinent data on checks was developed so that the data could be read electronically. The MICR system contributed significantly to the automation of check processing.

In the 1970s, the Federal Reserve introduced a regional check-processing program to further improve the efficiency of check clearing, which resulted in an increase in the number of check-processing facilities throughout the country. In response to the recent decline in overall check usage, the

Reserve Banks began an initiative to better align Reserve Bank check-processing operations with the changing demand for those services. As part of the initiative, the Reserve Banks standardized check processing, consolidated some operations, and reduced the overall number of their check-processing sites.

Other improvements in check collection have focused on when a customer has access to funds deposited in a bank. Until the late 1980s, depository institutions were not required to make funds from check deposits available for withdrawal within specific time frames. In 1988, the Federal Reserve Board adopted Regulation CC, Availability of Funds and Collection of Checks, which implemented the Expedited Funds Availability Act. Regulation CC established maximum permissible hold periods for checks and other deposits, after which banks must make funds available for withdrawal. It also established rules to speed the return of unpaid checks. In late 1992, the Federal Reserve Board amended Regulation CC to permit all depository institutions to demand settlement in same-day funds from paying banks without paying presentment fees, provided presenting banks meet certain conditions.

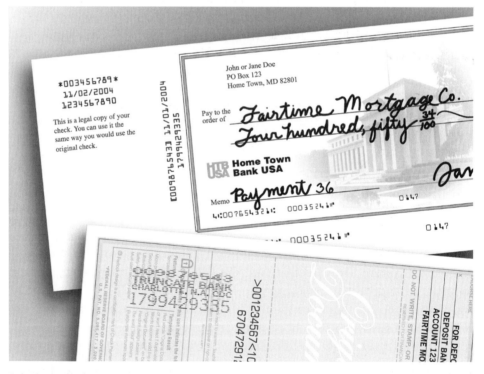

Substitute check

In addition to processing paper checks more efficiently, the Federal Reserve has also encouraged check truncation, which improves efficiency by eliminating the need to transfer paper checks physically between institutions. To that end, the Federal Reserve worked with Congress on the Check Clearing for the 21st Century Act, commonly known as Check 21, which became effective October 28, 2004. Check 21 facilitates check truncation by creating a new negotiable instrument called a substitute check, which is the legal equivalent of an original check. A substitute check is a paper reproduction of an original check that contains an image of the front and back of the original check and is suitable for automated processing, just as the original check is. Check 21 allows depository institutions to truncate original checks, process check information electronically, and deliver substitute checks to depository institutions if they require paper checks. In 2004, the Board amended Regulation CC to implement Check 21.

The Automated Clearinghouse

The automated clearinghouse (ACH) is an electronic payment system, developed jointly by the private sector and the Federal Reserve in the early 1970s as a more-efficient alternative to checks. Since then, the ACH has evolved into a nationwide mechanism that processes credit and debit transfers electronically. ACH credit transfers are used to make direct deposit payroll payments and corporate payments to vendors. ACH debit transfers are used by consumers to authorize the payment of insurance premiums, mortgages, loans, and other bills from their account. The ACH is also used by businesses to concentrate funds at a primary bank and to make payments to other businesses. In 2003, the Reserve Banks processed 6.5 billion ACH payments with a value of $16.8 trillion (table 7.5).

Table 7.5

Number and value of ACH transactions processed by the Reserve Banks, selected years, 1975–2003

Number in millions; value in millions of dollars

Year	Number	Value
1975	6	92,868
1980	227	286,600
1990	1,435	4,660,476
2000	4,651	14,024,445
2003	6,502	16,761,883

The use of the ACH has evolved over time. The ACH is now used to make certain payments initiated by telephone or over the Internet. In addition, merchants that receive checks at the point of sale and banks that receive bill-payment checks in the mail are increasingly converting those checks into ACH payments.

In 2001, the Reserve Banks began a cross-border ACH service. Legal and operational differences between countries have presented challenges to the rapid growth of the cross-border service; however, the Reserve Banks are continuing to work with financial institutions and ACH operators in other nations to address these challenges.

Depository institutions transmit ACH payments to the Reserve Banks in batches, rather than individually. ACH funds transfers are generally processed within one to two days, according to designated schedules, and are delivered to receiving institutions several times a day, as they are processed. The Reserve Banks offer ACH operator services to all depository institutions. A private-sector processor also provides ACH operator services in competition with the Reserve Banks. The Reserve Banks and the private-sector operator deliver ACH payments to participants in each other's system in order to maintain a national ACH payment system.

Both the government and the commercial sectors use ACH payments. Compared with checks, ACH transfers are less costly to process and provide greater certainty of payment to the receiver. Initially, the federal government was the dominant user of the ACH and promoted its use for Social Security and payroll payments. Since the early 1980s, commercial ACH volume has grown rapidly, and in 2003 it accounted for 86 percent of total ACH volume (table 7.6).

Table 7.6

ACH volume by type, selected years 1975–2003

Number in millions

Year	Number of commercial payments	Number of government payments	Commercial payments as a percentage of total (percent)
1975	5.8	.2	97
1980	64.5	162.5	28
1990	915.3	519.5	64
2000	3,812.0	839.0	82
2003	5,588.0	914.0	86

Wholesale Services

Fedwire Funds Service

The Fedwire Funds Service provides a real-time gross settlement system in which more than 9,500 participants are able to initiate electronic funds transfers that are immediate, final, and irrevocable. Depository institutions that maintain an account with a Reserve Bank are eligible to use the service to send payments directly to, or receive payments from, other participants. Depository institutions can also use a correspondent relationship with a Fedwire participant to make or receive transfers indirectly through the system. Participants generally use Fedwire to handle large-value, time-critical payments, such as payments to settle interbank purchases and sales of federal funds; to purchase, sell, or finance securities transactions; to disburse or repay large loans; and to settle real estate transactions. The Department of the Treasury, other federal agencies, and government-sponsored enterprises also use the Fedwire Funds Service to disburse and collect funds. In 2003, the Reserve Banks processed 123 million Fedwire payments having a total value of $436.7 trillion (table 7.7).

Table 7.7

Number and value of Fedwire funds transactions processed by the Federal Reserve, selected years, 1920–2003

Number in millions; value in millions of dollars

Year	Number	Value
1920	.5	30,857
1930	1.9	198,881
1940	.8	92,106
1950	1.0	509,168
1960	3.0	2,428,083
1970	7.0	12,332,001
1980	43.0	78,594,862
1990	62.6	199,067,200
2000	108.3	379,756,389
2003	123.0	436,706,269

Fedwire funds transfers are processed individually, rather than in batches as ACH transfers are. The Federal Reserve uses secure, sophisticated data-communications and data-processing systems to ensure that each transfer is authorized by the sender and that it is not altered while it is under the control of a Reserve Bank. Although a few depository institutions use the telephone to initiate Fedwire payments, more than 99 percent of all Fedwire funds transfers are initiated electronically. The Federal Reserve processes Fedwire funds transfers in seconds, electronically debiting the account of the sending institution and crediting the account of the receiving institution. The Federal Reserve guarantees the payment, assuming any risk that the institution sending the payment has insufficient funds in its Federal Reserve account to complete the transfer.

Fedwire Securities Service

The Fedwire Securities Service provides safekeeping, transfer, and settlement services for securities issued by the Treasury, federal agencies, government-sponsored enterprises, and certain international organizations. The Reserve Banks perform these services as fiscal agents for these entities. Securities are safekept in the form of electronic records of securities held in custody accounts. Securities are transferred according to instructions provided by parties with access to the system. Access to the Fedwire Securities Service is limited to depository institutions that maintain accounts with a Reserve Bank, and a few other organizations, such as federal agencies, government-sponsored enterprises, and state government treasurer's offices (which are designated by the U.S. Treasury to hold securities accounts). Other parties, specifically brokers and dealers, typically hold and transfer securities through depository institutions that are Fedwire participants and that provide specialized government securities clearing services. In 2003, the Fedwire Securities Service processed 20.4 million securities transfers with a value of $267.6 trillion (table 7.8).

Table 7.8

Number and value of book-entry securities transfers processed by the Federal Reserve, selected years, 1970–2003

Number in millions; value in millions of dollars

Year	Number	Value
1970	.3	258,200
1980	4.1	13,354,100
1990	10.9	99,861,205
2000	13.6	188,133,178
2003	20.4	267,644,194

Fedwire securities are processed individually, in much the same way that Fedwire funds transfers are processed, and participants initiate securities transfers in the same manner, using either a computer connection or the telephone. When the Federal Reserve receives a request to transfer a security, for example as a result of the sale of securities, it determines that the security is held in safekeeping for the institution requesting the transfer and withdraws the security from the institution's safekeeping account. It then electronically credits the proceeds of the sale to the account of the depository institution, deposits the book-entry security into the safekeeping account of the receiving institution, and electronically debits that institution's account for the purchase price. Most securities transfers involve the delivery of securities and the simultaneous exchange of payment, which is referred to as delivery versus payment. The transfer of securities ownership and related funds is final at the time of transfer, and the Federal Reserve guarantees payment to institutions that initiate such securities transfers.

National Settlement Service

The National Settlement Service allows participants in private-sector clearing arrangements to do multilateral funds settlements on a net basis using balances in their Federal Reserve accounts. The service provides an automated mechanism for submitting settlement information to the Reserve Banks. It improves operational efficiency and controls for this process and reduces settlement risk to participants by granting settlement finality for movements of funds on settlement day. The service also enables the Federal Reserve to manage and limit the financial risk posed by these arrangements because it incorporates risk controls that are as stringent as those used in the Fedwire Funds Service. Approximately seventy arrangements use the National Settlement Service—primarily check clearinghouse associations, but also other types of arrangements.

Fiscal Agency Services

As fiscal agents of the United States, the Reserve Banks function as the U.S. government's bank and perform a variety of services for the Treasury, other government agencies, government-sponsored enterprises, and some international organizations. Often the fiscal agent services performed by the Reserve Banks are the same, or similar to, services that the Reserve Banks provide to the banking system. Services performed for the Treasury include maintaining the Treasury's bank account; processing payments; and issuing, safekeeping, and transferring securities. Fiscal services performed for other entities are generally securities-related. The Treasury and other entities reimburse the Reserve Banks for the expenses incurred in providing these services.

As fiscal agents of the United States, the Reserve Banks function as the U.S. government's bank.

One of the unique fiscal agency functions that the Reserve Banks provide to the Treasury is a program through which the Reserve Banks invest Treasury monies until needed to fund the government's operations. The Treasury receives funds from two principal sources: tax receipts and borrowings. The funds that flow into and out of the government's account vary in amount throughout the year; for example, the account balance tends to be relatively high during the April tax season. The Treasury directs the Reserve Banks to invest funds in excess of a previously agreed-upon minimum amount in special collateralized accounts at depository institutions nationwide. The Federal Reserve monitors these balances for compliance with collateral requirements and returns the funds to the Treasury when they are needed.

This investment facility, in which excess funds are invested in accounts at depository institutions, also facilitates the implementation of monetary policy. When funds flow from depository institutions into the Treasury's account at the Federal Reserve, the supply of Federal Reserve balances to depository institutions decreases. The reverse occurs when funds flow from the Treasury's Federal Reserve account to the Treasury's accounts at depository institutions. A stable balance in the Treasury's account at the Federal Reserve mitigates the effect of Treasury's receipts and disbursements on the supply of Federal Reserve balances to depository institutions.

The Reserve Banks make disbursements from the government's account through Fedwire funds transfers or ACH payments, or to a limited extent, by check. Fedwire disbursements are typically associated with, but not limited to, the redemption of Treasury securities. Certain recurring transactions, such as Social Security benefit payments and government employee salary payments, are processed mainly by the ACH and electronically deposited directly to the recipients' accounts at their depository institutions. Other government payments may be made using Treasury checks drawn on the government's account at the Reserve Banks. The Treasury continues to work to move the remaining government payments away from Treasury checks toward electronic payments, primarily the ACH, in an effort to improve efficiency and reduce the costs associated with government payments.

The Federal Reserve plays an important role when the Treasury needs to raise money to finance the government or to refinance maturing Treasury securities. The Reserve Banks handle weekly, monthly, and quarterly auctions of Treasury securities, accepting bids, communicating them to the Treasury, issuing the securities in book-entry form to the winning bidders, and collecting payment for the securities. Over the past several years, the auction process has become increasingly automated, which further ensures a smooth borrowing process. For example, automation has reduced to only minutes the time between the close of bidding and the announcement of the results of a Treasury securities auction.

Treasury securities are maintained in book-entry form in either the Reserve Banks' Fedwire Securities Service or the Treasury's TreasuryDirect system, which is also operated by the Reserve Banks. Even though TreasuryDirect holds less than 2 percent of all outstanding Treasury securities, it provides a convenient way for individuals to hold their securities directly, rather than with a third party such as a depository institution. Individuals purchase Treasury securities either directly from the Treasury when they are issued or on the secondary market, and they instruct their broker that the securities be delivered to their TreasuryDirect account. Once the securities are deposited there, the ACH directly deposits any interest or principal payments owed to the account holder to the account holder's account at a depository institution. A Reserve Bank, if requested, will sell securities held in TreasuryDirect for a fee on the secondary market, even though this is a service intended for individuals who hold Treasury securities to maturity.

The Federal Reserve also provides support for the Treasury's savings bonds program. Although savings bonds represent less than 5 percent of the federal debt, they are a means for individuals to invest in government securities with a small initial investment, currently $25. The Reserve Banks issue, service, and redeem tens of millions of U.S. savings bonds each year on behalf of the Treasury. As authorized by the Treasury, the Reserve Banks also qualify depository institutions and corporations to serve as issuing agents and paying agents for savings bonds. [3]

International Services

As the central bank of the United States, the Federal Reserve performs services for foreign central banks and for international organizations such as the International Monetary Fund and the International Bank for Reconstruction and Development. The Reserve Banks provide several types of services to these organizations, including maintaining non-interest-bearing deposit accounts (in U.S. dollars), securities safekeeping accounts, and accounts for safekeeping gold. Some foreign official institutions direct a portion of their daily receipts and payments in U.S. dollars through their funds accounts at the Federal Reserve. If an account contains excess funds, the foreign official institution may request that these funds be invested overnight in repurchase agreements with the Reserve Banks. If investments are needed for longer periods, the foreign official institution may provide instructions to buy securities to be held in safekeeping. Conversely, the foreign institution may provide instructions to sell securities held in safekeeping, with the proceeds deposited in its account. The Reserve Banks charge foreign official institutions for these services.

Gold vault, Federal Reserve Bank of New York

Federal Reserve Intraday Credit Policy

Each day, the Reserve Banks process a large number of payment transactions resulting from the Banks' role in providing payment services to depository institutions. Because depository institutions in the aggregate generally hold a relatively small amount of funds overnight in their Reserve Bank accounts, the Reserve Banks extend intraday credit, commonly referred to as daylight credit or daylight-overdraft credit, to facilitate the settlement of payment transactions and to ensure the smooth functioning of the U.S. payments system. To address the risk of providing this credit, the Federal Reserve has developed a policy that balances the goals of ensuring smooth functioning of the payments system and managing the Federal Reserve's direct credit risk from institutions' use of Federal Reserve intraday credit.

---

3. Savings bonds are now available in book-entry form from the Treasury, through www.TreasuryDirect.gov.

Institutions incur daylight overdrafts in their Reserve Bank accounts because of the mismatch in timing between the settlement of payments owed and the settlement of payments due. The Federal Reserve uses a schedule of rules, referred to as daylight-overdraft posting rules, to determine whether a daylight overdraft has occurred in an institution's account. The daylight-overdraft posting rules define the time of day that debits and credits for transactions processed by the Reserve Banks will be posted to an institution's account. The Federal Reserve relies on an automated system to measure an institution's intraday account activity, to monitor its compliance with the Federal Reserve's policy, and to calculate the institution's daylight-overdraft charges. The Reserve Banks' daylight-overdraft exposure can be significant. For example, in 2003 daylight overdrafts across depository institutions peaked at levels over $100 billion per day (chart 7.2).

Chart 7.2

Average peak daylight overdrafts of depository institutions, 1986:Q1–2004:Q2

Billions of dollars

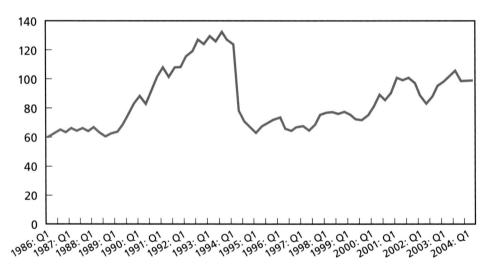

NOTE: The Federal Reserve measures each depository institution's account balance at the end of each minute during the business day. An institution's peak daylight overdraft for a given day is its largest negative end-of-minute balance. The System peak daylight overdraft for a given day is determined by adding the negative account balances of all depository institutions at the end of each minute and then selecting the largest negative end-of-minute balance. The quarterly average peak is the sum of daily System peaks for a quarter divided by the number of days in that quarter.

The Federal Reserve's policy establishes various measures to control the risks associated with daylight overdrafts. Beginning in 1985, the policy set a maximum limit, or net debit cap, on depository institutions' daylight-overdraft positions. In order to adopt a net debit cap greater than zero, an institution must be in sound financial condition. Certain institutions may be eligible to obtain additional daylight-overdraft capacity above their net debit caps by pledging collateral, subject to Reserve Bank approval. Institutions must have regular access to the Federal Reserve's discount window so that they can borrow overnight from their Reserve Bank to cover any daylight overdrafts that are not eliminated before the end of the day. Those that lack regular access to the discount window are prohibited from incurring daylight overdrafts in their Reserve Bank accounts and are subject to additional risk controls. Beginning in 1994, the Reserve Banks also began charging fees to depository institutions for their use of daylight overdrafts as an economic incentive to reduce the overdrafts, thereby reducing direct Federal Reserve credit risk and contributing to economic efficiency.

Federal Reserve policy allows Reserve Banks to apply additional risk controls to an account holder's payment activity, if necessary to limit risk. These risk controls include unilaterally reducing an account holder's net debit cap, placing real-time controls on the account holder's payment activity so that requested payments are rejected, or requiring the account holder to pledge collateral to cover its daylight overdrafts.

A   **Extensions of Credit by Federal Reserve Banks**
Governs borrowing by depository institutions and others at the
Federal Reserve discount window

B   **Equal Credit Opportunity**
Prohibits lenders from discriminating against credit applicants,
establishes guidelines for gathering and evaluating credit information, and requires written notification when credit is denied

C   **Home Mortgage Disclosure**
Requires certain mortgage lenders to disclose data regarding their
lending patterns

D   **Reserve Requirements of Depository Institutions**
Sets uniform requirements for all depository institutions to maintain reserves either with their Federal Reserve Bank or as cash in
their vaults

E   **Electronic Funds Transfers**
Establishes the rights, liabilities, and responsibilities of parties in
electronic funds transfers and protects consumers when they use
such systems

F   **Limitations on Interbank Liabilities**
Prescribes standards to limit the risks that the failure of a depository institution would pose to an insured depository institution

G   **Disclosure and Reporting of CRA-Related Agreements**
Implements provisions of the Gramm-Leach-Bliley Act that
require reporting and public disclosure of written agreements
between (1) insured depository institutions or their affiliates and
(2) nongovernmental entities or persons, made in connection with
fulfillment of Community Reinvestment Act requirements

H   **Membership of State Banking Institutions
in the Federal Reserve System**
Defines the requirements for membership of state-chartered banks
in the Federal Reserve System; sets limitations on certain investments and requirements for certain types of loans; describes rules
pertaining to securities-related activities; establishes the minimum
ratios of capital to assets that banks must maintain and procedures

for prompt corrective action when banks are not adequately capitalized; prescribes real estate lending and appraisal standards; sets out requirements concerning bank security procedures, suspicious-activity reports, and compliance with the Bank Secrecy Act; and establishes rules governing banks' ownership or control of financial subsidiaries

I **Issue and Cancellation of Capital Stock of Federal Reserve Banks**
Sets out stock-subscription requirements for all banks joining the Federal Reserve System

J **Collection of Checks and Other Items by Federal Reserve Banks and Funds Transfers through Fedwire**
Establishes procedures, duties, and responsibilities among (1) Federal Reserve Banks, (2) the senders and payors of checks and other items, and (3) the senders and recipients of Fedwire funds transfers

K **International Banking Operations**
Governs the international banking operations of U.S. banking organizations and the operations of foreign banks in the United States

L **Management Official Interlocks**
Generally prohibits a management official from serving two non-affiliated depository institutions, depository institution holding companies, or any combination thereof, in situations where the management interlock would likely have an anticompetitive effect

M **Consumer Leasing**
Implements the consumer leasing provisions of the Truth in Lending Act by requiring meaningful disclosure of leasing terms

N **Relations with Foreign Banks and Bankers**
Governs relationships and transactions between Federal Reserve Banks and foreign banks, bankers, or governments

O **Loans to Executive Officers, Directors, and Principal Shareholders of Member Banks**
Restricts credit that a member bank may extend to its executive officers, directors, and principal shareholders and their related interests

P **Privacy of Consumer Financial Information**
Governs how financial institutions use nonpublic personal information about consumers

Q   **Prohibition against Payment of Interest on Demand Deposits**
Prohibits member banks from paying interest on demand deposits

S   **Reimbursement to Financial Institutions for Assembling or Providing Financial Records; Recordkeeping Requirements for Certain Financial Records**
Establishes rates and conditions for reimbursement to financial institutions for providing customer records to a government authority and prescribes recordkeeping and reporting requirements for insured depository institutions making domestic wire transfers and for insured depository institutions and nonbank financial institutions making international wire transfers

T   **Credit by Brokers and Dealers**
Governs extension of credit by securities brokers and dealers, including all members of national securities exchanges (See also Regulations U and X.)

U   **Credit by Banks and Persons Other Than Brokers and Dealers for the Purpose of Purchasing or Carrying Margin Stock**
Governs extension of credit by banks or persons other than brokers or dealers to finance the purchase or the carrying of margin securities (See also Regulations T and X.)

V   **Fair Credit Reporting**
Implements the provisions of the Fair Credit Reporting Act applicable to financial institutions regarding obtaining and using consumer reports and other information about consumers, sharing such information among affiliates, furnishing information to consumer reporting agencies, and preventing identity theft

W   **Transactions Between Member Banks and Their Affiliates**
Implements sections 23A and 23B of the Federal Reserve Act, which establish certain restrictions on and requirements for transactions between a member bank and its affiliates

X   **Borrowers of Securities Credit**
Applies the provisions of Regulations T and U to borrowers who are subject to U.S. laws and who obtain credit within or outside the United States for the purpose of purchasing securities

Y   **Bank Holding Companies and Change in Bank Control**
Regulates the acquisition of control of banks and bank holding companies by companies and individuals, defines and regulates the nonbanking activities in which bank holding companies (includ-

ing financial holding companies) and foreign banking organizations with United States operations may engage, and establishes the minimum ratios of capital to assets that bank holding companies must maintain

Z   Truth in Lending
Prescribes uniform methods for computing the cost of credit, for disclosing credit terms, and for resolving errors on certain types of credit accounts

AA   Unfair or Deceptive Acts or Practices
Establishes consumer complaint procedures and defines unfair or deceptive practices in extending credit to consumers

BB   Community Reinvestment
Implements the Community Reinvestment Act and encourages banks to help meet the credit needs of their entire communities

CC   Availability of Funds and Collection of Checks
Governs the availability of funds deposited in checking accounts and the collection and return of checks

DD   Truth in Savings
Requires depository institutions to provide disclosures to enable consumers to make meaningful comparisons of deposit accounts

EE   Netting Eligibility for Financial Institutions
Defines financial institutions to be covered by statutory provisions that validate netting contracts, thereby permitting one institution to pay or receive the net, rather than the gross, amount due, even if the other institution is insolvent

This glossary gives basic definitions of terms used in the text. Readers looking for more comprehensive explanations may want to consult textbooks in economics, banking, and finance.

A

agreement corporation

Corporation chartered by a state to engage in international banking; so named because the corporation enters into an "agreement" with the Board of Governors to limit its activities to those permitted an Edge Act corporation. Typically organized as a subsidiary of a bank, an agreement corporation may conduct activities abroad that are permissible to foreign banks abroad but that may not otherwise be permissible for U.S. banks.

automated clearinghouse (ACH)

Electronic clearing and settlement system for exchanging electronic credit and debit transactions among participating depository institutions. The Federal Reserve Banks operate an automated clearinghouse, as do private organizations.

B

balances

See **Federal Reserve balances**.

Bank for International Settlements (BIS)

International organization established in 1930 and based in Basel, Switzerland, that serves as a forum for central banks for collecting information, developing analyses, and cooperating on a wide range of policy-related matters; also provides certain financial services to central banks.

bank holding company

Company that owns, or has controlling interest in, one or more banks. The Board of Governors is responsible for regulating and supervising bank holding companies, even if the bank owned by the holding company is under the primary supervision of a different federal agency (the Comptroller of the Currency or the Federal Deposit Insurance Corporation).

Bank Holding Company Act of 1956

Federal legislation that establishes the legal framework under which bank holding companies operate and places the formation of bank holding companies and their acquisition of banking and nonbanking interests under the supervision of the Federal Reserve.

banking organization
A bank holding company (consolidated to include all of its subsidiary banks and nonbank subsidiaries) or an independent bank (a bank that is not owned or controlled by a bank holding company).

bank regulation
Actions to make and issue rules and regulations and enforce those rules and other laws governing the structure and conduct of banking.

bank supervision
Oversight of individual banks to ensure that they are operated prudently and in accordance with applicable statutes and regulations.

Basel Committee on Banking Supervision
An international committee of bank supervisors, associated with the BIS, that is headquartered in Basel, Switzerland, and is composed of bank supervisors from Belgium, Canada, France, Germany, Italy, Japan, Luxembourg, the Netherlands, Spain, Sweden, Switzerland, the United Kingdom, and the United States.

Basel I
Informal name for the 1988 agreement—the International Convergence of Capital Measurement and Capital Standards—under which national bank supervisors for the first time agreed on an international framework for capital adequacy guidelines. Also known as the Basel Accord.

Basel II
Informal name for the 2004 agreement updating the Basel Accord. Also known as the New Basel Accord, Basel II has three pillars: minimum capital requirements, supervisory oversight, and market discipline.

Board of Governors
Central, governmental agency of the Federal Reserve System, located in Washington, D.C., and composed of seven members, who are appointed by the President and confirmed by the Senate. The Board, with other components of the System, has responsibilities associated with the conduct of monetary policy, the supervision and regulation of certain banking organizations, the operation of much of the nation's payments system, and the administration of many federal laws that protect consumers in credit transactions. The Board also supervises the Federal Reserve Banks.

book-entry securities

Securities that are recorded in electronic records, called book entries, rather than as paper certificates. (*Compare* **definitive securities**.)

C

Call Report

Informal name for quarterly Reports of Condition and Income.

capital

In banking, the funds invested in a bank that are available to absorb loan losses or other problems and therefore protect depositors. Capital includes all equity and some types of debt. Bank regulators have developed two definitions of capital for supervisory purposes: tier 1 capital, which can absorb losses while a bank continues operating, and tier 2 capital, which may be of limited life and may carry an interest obligation or other characteristics of a debt obligation, and therefore provides less protection to depositors than tier 1 capital.

capital market

The market in which corporate equity and longer-term debt securities (those maturing in more than one year) are issued and traded. (*Compare* **money market**.)

cash

U.S. paper currency plus coin.

central bank

Principal monetary authority of a nation, which performs several key functions, including conducting monetary policy to stabilize the economy and level of prices. The Federal Reserve is the central bank of the United States.

check clearing

The movement of a check from the depository institution at which it was deposited back to the institution on which it was written, the movement of funds in the opposite direction, and the corresponding credit and debit to the accounts involved. Check clearing also encompasses the return of a check (for insufficient funds, for example) from the bank on which it was written to the bank at which it was deposited, and the corresponding movement of funds. The Federal Reserve Banks operate a nationwide check-clearing system.

check truncation
The practice of removing an original paper check from the check-clearing process and sending in its place an alternative paper or electronic version of the essential information on the check.

clearing
General term that may refer to check clearing or to the process of matching trades between the sellers and buyers of securities and other financial instruments and contracts.

commercial bank
Bank that offers a variety of deposit accounts, including checking, savings, and time deposits, and extends loans to individuals and businesses. Commercial banks can be contrasted with investment banking firms, which generally are involved in arranging for the sale of corporate or municipal securities, and broker-dealer firms, which buy and sell securities for themselves and others. (*Compare* **savings bank**.)

commercial paper
Short-term, unsecured promissory note issued by an industrial or commercial firm, a financial company, or a foreign government.

Consumer Advisory Council
Group, created under the Federal Reserve Act, composed of thirty members who represent the interests of a broad range of consumers and creditors. The council meets with the Board of Governors three times a year on matters concerning consumers and the consumer protection laws administered by the Board.

corporate bond
Interest-bearing or discounted debt obligation issued by a private corporation.

contractual clearing balance
An amount a depository institution may contract to maintain in its account at a Federal Reserve Bank in addition to any reserve balance requirement. This amount helps ensure that the institution can meet its daily transaction obligations without overdrawing its account. Balances maintained to satisfy the contractual clearing balance earn credits that can be used to pay for services provided by the Federal Reserve Banks.

correspondent bank
Bank that accepts the deposits of, and performs services for, another bank (called a respondent bank).

credit risk

The risk that economic loss will result from the failure of an obligor to repay financial institutions according to the terms and conditions of a contract or agreement.

credit union

Financial cooperative organization whose membership consists of individuals who have a common bond, such as place of employment or residence or membership in a labor union. Credit unions accept deposits from members, pay interest (in the form of dividends) on the deposits out of earnings, and use their funds mainly to provide consumer installment loans to members.

currency

Paper money that consists mainly of Federal Reserve notes. Other types of currency that were once issued by the United States include silver certificates, United States notes, and national bank notes.

D

daylight overdraft

A negative balance in an institution's Federal Reserve Bank account at any time during the operating hours of the Fedwire Funds Service.

daylight-overdraft posting rules

A schedule used to determine the timing of debits and credits to an institution's Federal Reserve Bank account for various transactions processed by the Reserve Banks.

definitive securities

Securities that are recorded on engraved paper certificates and payable to the bearers or to specific, registered owners. (*Compare* **book-entry securities**.)

demand deposit

A deposit that the depositor has a right to withdraw at any time without prior notice to the depository institution. By law, no interest can be paid on such deposits. Demand deposits are commonly offered in the form of checking accounts.

depository institution

Financial institution that makes loans and obtains its funds mainly through accepting deposits from the public; includes commercial banks, savings and loan associations, savings banks, and credit unions.

derivative

A financial instrument whose value depends upon the characteristics and value of an underlying commodity, currency, or security.

discounting

Practice of extending credit in which the borrower endorses a negotiable instrument or other commercial paper in the borrower's portfolio over to the lender in exchange for funds from the lender in the amount of the instrument's face value less the interest due over the term of the loan, that is, the "discounted" value.

discount rate

Officially the primary credit rate, it is the interest rate at which an eligible depository institution may borrow funds, typically for a short period, directly from a Federal Reserve Bank. The law requires that the board of directors of each Reserve Bank establish the discount rate every fourteen days, subject to review and determination by the Board of Governors.

discount window (the window)

Figurative expression for the Federal Reserve facility that extends credit directly to eligible depository institutions (those subject to reserve requirements); so named because, in the early days of the Federal Reserve System, bankers would come to a Reserve Bank teller window to obtain credit.

discount window credit

Credit extended by a Federal Reserve Bank to an eligible depository institution. All discount window borrowing must be secured by collateral. Three types of discount window credit are available to eligible depository institutions:

- **primary credit**

   Credit extended to generally sound depository institutions at a rate above the target federal funds rate on a very short-term basis as a backup source of funding.

- **seasonal credit**

   Credit extended by a Federal Reserve Bank to depository institutions that have difficulty raising funds in national money markets to help meet temporary needs for funds resulting from regular, seasonal fluctuations in loans and deposits. The interest rate charged is based on market rates.

- **secondary credit**

   Credit extended to depository institutions ineligible for primary credit, at a rate above the primary credit rate, either on a very short-term basis (when consistent with a timely return to market sources of funds) or for a longer term (to facilitate the orderly resolution of serious financial difficulties).

E

easing

Federal Reserve action to lower the federal funds rate. The action is undertaken when economic activity needs to be stimulated. (*Compare* **tightening**.)

Edge Act corporation (or Edge corporation)

Corporation chartered by the Federal Reserve to engage in international banking. The Board of Governors acts on applications to establish Edge Act corporations and also examines the corporations and their subsidiaries. Typically organized as a subsidiary of a bank, an Edge Act corporation may conduct activities abroad that are permissible to foreign banks abroad but that may not otherwise be permissible to U.S. banks. Named after Senator Walter Edge of New Jersey, who sponsored the original legislation to permit formation of such organizations. (*Compare* **agreement corporation**.)

elastic currency

Currency that can, by the actions of the central monetary authority, expand or contract in amount warranted by economic conditions.

electronic funds transfer (EFT)

Transfer of funds electronically rather than by check or cash. The Federal Reserve's Fedwire Funds Service and automated clearinghouse services are EFT systems. (EFTs subject to the Electronic Funds Transfer Act are more narrowly defined.)

Eurocurrency liabilities

A generic term referring to liabilities in a bank located in a country other than the one that issues the currency in which the liability is denominated. Despite its name, Eurocurrency need not be a liability of a European banking office nor denominated in European currency. Not to be confused with the euro, the name of the common currency of twelve (as of 2004) European Union countries.

Eurodollar deposits

Dollar-denominated deposits in banks and other financial institutions outside the United States; includes deposits at banks not only in Europe, but in all parts of the world.

excess reserves

Amount of funds held by an institution in its account at a Federal Reserve Bank in excess of its required reserve balance and its contractual clearing balance.

F

Federal Advisory Council

Advisory group made up of one representative (in most cases a banker) from each of the twelve Federal Reserve Districts. Established by the Federal Reserve Act, the council meets periodically with the Board of Governors to discuss business and financial conditions and to make recommendations.

federal agency securities

Interest-bearing obligations issued by federal agencies and government-sponsored entities, such as the Federal Home Loan Banks, the Federal Farm Credit Banks, the Federal National Mortgage Association (Fannie Mae), the Federal Home Loan Mortgage Corporation (Freddie Mac), and the Tennessee Valley Authority. Some federal agency securities are backed by the U.S. government while others are not.

Federal Financial Institutions Examination Council (FFIEC)

Group of representatives of the federal banking regulatory agencies—the Board of Governors, the Office of Thrift Supervision, the Federal Deposit Insurance Corporation, the Office of the Comptroller of the Currency, and the National Credit Union Administration—established to help maintain uniform standards for examining and supervising federally insured depository institutions.

federal funds transactions

Short-term transactions in immediately available funds—between depository institutions and certain other institutions that maintain accounts with the Federal Reserve—that involve lending balances at the Federal Reserve; usually not collateralized.

federal funds rate

Rate charged by a depository institution on an overnight loan of federal funds to another depository institution; rate may vary from day to day and from bank to bank.

Federal Open Market Committee (FOMC, or the Committee)

Twelve-voting-member committee made up of the seven members of the Board of Governors; the president of the Federal Reserve Bank of New York; and, on a rotating basis, the presidents of four other Reserve Banks. Nonvoting Reserve Bank presidents also participate in Committee deliberations and discussion. The FOMC generally meets eight times a year in Washington, D.C., to set the nation's monetary policy. It also establishes policy relating to System operations in the foreign exchange markets.

Federal Reserve Act

Federal legislation, enacted in 1913, that established the Federal Reserve System.

Federal Reserve balances

The amount of funds held by a depository institution in its account at its Federal Reserve Bank.

Federal Reserve Bank

One of the twelve operating arms of the Federal Reserve System, located throughout the nation, that together with their Branches carry out various System functions, including providing payment services to depository institutions, distributing the nation's currency and coin, supervising and regulating member banks and bank holding companies, and serving as fiscal agent for the U.S. government.

Federal Reserve District (Reserve District, or District)

One of the twelve geographic regions served by a Federal Reserve Bank.

Federal Reserve float

Float is credit that appears on the books of the depository institution of both the check writer (the payor) and the check receiver (the payee) while a check is being processed. Federal Reserve float is float present during the Federal Reserve Banks' check-clearing process. To promote efficiency in the payments system and provide certainty about the date that deposited funds will become available to the receiving depository institution (and the payee), the Federal Reserve Banks credit the accounts of banks that deposit checks according to a fixed schedule. However, processing certain checks and collecting funds from the banks on which these checks are written may take more time than the schedule allows. Therefore, the accounts of some banks may be credited before the Federal Reserve Banks are able to collect payment from other banks, resulting in Federal Reserve float.

Federal Reserve note

Paper currency issued by the Federal Reserve Banks. Nearly all the nation's circulating currency is in the form of Federal Reserve notes, which are printed by the Bureau of Engraving and Printing, a bureau of the U.S. Department of the Treasury. Federal Reserve notes are obligations of the Federal Reserve Banks and legal tender for all debts.

Federal Reserve Regulatory Service

Monthly subscription service that includes all statutes and regulations for which the Federal Reserve has responsibility, Board of Governors interpretations and rulings, official staff commentaries, significant staff opinions, and procedural rules under which the Board operates.

Federal Reserve System

The central bank of the United States, created by the Federal Reserve Act and made up of a seven-member Board of Governors in Washington, D.C., twelve regional Federal Reserve Banks, and Branches of the Federal Reserve Banks.

Fedwire Funds Service

Electronic funds transfer network operated by the Federal Reserve Banks. It is usually used to transfer large amounts of funds from one institution's account at the Federal Reserve to another institution's account. It is also used by the U.S. Department of the Treasury, other federal agencies, and government-sponsored enterprises to collect and disburse funds.

Fedwire Securities Service

Electronic vault that stores records of book-entry securities holdings and a transfer and settlement mechanism used by depository institutions to transfer custody of book-entry securities from one depository institution to another. The securities on the Fedwire Securities Service include U.S. Treasury securities, U.S. agency securities, mortgage-backed securities issued by government-sponsored enterprises, and securities of certain international organizations.

financial holding company

A bank holding company that has met the capital, managerial, and other requirements to take advantage of the expanded affiliations allowed under the Gramm-Leach-Bliley Act.

financial institution

Institution that uses its funds chiefly to purchase financial assets, such as loans or securities (as opposed to tangible assets, such as real estate). Financial institutions can be separated into two major groups according to the nature of the principal claims they issue: (1) depository institutions (also called depository intermediaries), such as commercial banks, savings and loan associations, savings banks, and credit unions, which obtain funds largely by accepting deposits from the public and (2) nondepositories (sometimes called nondepository intermediaries), such as life insurance and property–casualty insurance companies and pension funds, whose claims are the policies they sell or their promise to provide income after retirement.

fiscal agency services

Services performed by the Federal Reserve Banks for the U.S. government and other organizations, including maintaining accounts for the U.S. Department of the Treasury, paying checks and making electronic payments on behalf of the Treasury, and selling and redeeming marketable Treasury securities and savings bonds.

fiscal policy
Federal government policy regarding taxation and spending, set by Congress and the President.

flexible exchange rates
Arrangements in which the rate of exchange between countries' currencies (the foreign exchange rate) is allowed to fluctuate in response to market forces of supply and demand.

foreign currency operations
Transactions in the foreign exchange markets involving the purchase of the currency of one nation with that of another. Also called foreign exchange transactions.

foreign exchange intervention
A foreign currency operation (*see* above) designed to influence the value of the dollar against foreign currencies, typically with the aim of stabilizing disorderly markets.

foreign exchange markets
Markets in which foreign currencies are purchased and sold.

foreign exchange rate
Price of the currency of one nation in terms of the currency of another nation.

G

government securities
Securities issued by the U.S. Treasury or federal agencies.

Gramm-Leach-Bliley Act
Federal legislation that allowed affiliations among banks, securities firms, and insurance companies under a financial holding company structure. The act reaffirmed the Federal Reserve's role as "umbrella supervisor" over organizations that control banks, while also requiring that bank regulators and functional regulators supervise subsidiaries within a financial holding company.

gross domestic product (GDP)
Total value of goods and services produced by labor and property located in the United States during a specific period.

Group of Seven (G-7)

International group made up of seven leading industrial nations—Canada, France, Germany, Italy, Japan, the United Kingdom, and the United States—whose finance ministers and central bank governors meet occasionally to discuss economic policy.

I

interest-rate risk

Risk of gain or loss in the value of a portfolio as a result of changes in market interest rates.

international banking facility

Specially designated activities of a bank located in the United States that are treated as those of an offshore bank by U.S. regulatory authorities. Dollar deposits in such a facility are considered to be Eurodollars.

International Monetary Fund (IMF)

International organization established for lending funds to member nations to promote international monetary cooperation among nations, to facilitate the expansion and balanced growth of international trade, and to finance temporary balance-of-payments deficits, usually in conjunction with macroeconomic adjustment programs.

L

liquidity

Quality that makes an asset easily convertible into cash with relatively little loss of value in the conversion process. Sometimes used more broadly to encompass cash and credit in hand and promises of credit to meet needs for cash.

liquidity risk

In banking, the risk that a depository institution will not have sufficient cash or liquid assets to meet the claims of depositors and other creditors.

M

M1

Measure of the U.S. money stock that consists of currency held by the public, traveler's checks, demand deposits, and other checkable deposits.

M2

Measure of the U.S. money stock that consists of M1, savings deposits (including money market deposit accounts), time deposits in amounts of less than $100,000, and balances in retail money market mutual funds. Excludes individual retirement account (IRA) and Keough balances at depository institutions and retail money funds.

M3

Measure of the U.S. money stock that consists of M2, time deposits of $100,000 or more at all depository institutions, repurchase agreements in amounts of $100,000 or more, Eurodollars, and balances held in institutional money market mutual funds.

margin requirement

Buying on margin refers to buying stocks or securities with borrowed money (usually borrowed from a brokerage firm or bank). The margin requirement is the minimum amount (expressed as a percentage) the buyer must put up (rather than borrow). The Federal Reserve Board sets margin requirements.

market interest rates

Rates of interest determined by the interaction of the supply of and demand for funds in freely functioning markets.

market risk

The risk that a banking organization may incur losses due to the change in market value of an asset or liability on its balance sheet.

member bank

Depository institution that is a member of the Federal Reserve System. All national banks are automatically members of the System; state-chartered banks may choose to apply to join the System.

monetary aggregates

Aggregate measures through which the Federal Reserve monitors the nation's monetary assets: M1, M2, and M3.

monetary policy

A central bank's actions to influence the availability and cost of money and credit, as a means of helping to promote national economic goals. Tools of monetary policy include open market operations, direct lending to depository institutions, and reserve requirements.

monetize

Action in which a central bank purchases an object that is not money (for example, gold) and pays for it by creating balances at the central bank. The action permits an increase in the money stock.

money

Anything that serves as a generally accepted medium of exchange, a standard of value, and a means of saving or storing purchasing power. In the United States, currency (the bulk of which is Federal Reserve notes) and coin as well as funds in deposit accounts at depository institutions are examples of money.

money market

Figurative expression for the informal network of dealers and investors over which short-term debt securities are purchased and sold. Money market securities generally are highly liquid securities that mature in less than one year, often less than ninety days. (*Compare* **capital market**.)

money stock

Total quantity of money available for transactions and investment; measures of the U.S. money stock include M1, M2, and M3. (Also referred to as the money supply or, simply, money.)

mutual savings bank

Savings bank owned by its depositors (contrasted with a stock savings bank, which issues common stock to the public).

N

national bank

A commercial bank that is chartered by the Office of the Comptroller of the Currency, which is a bureau of the U.S. Department of the Treasury; by law, national banks are members of the Federal Reserve System.

net debit cap

The maximum uncollateralized daylight-overdraft position that a depository institution is permitted to incur in its Federal Reserve Bank account at any point in the day, or on average over a two-week period.

nominal interest rates

Current stated rates of interest paid or earned. (*Compare* **real interest rates**.)

nonmember bank

State-chartered commercial bank that is not a member of the Federal Reserve System.

nonpersonal time deposit

Time deposit held by a depositor other than an individual (for example, a corporation).

O

official foreign exchange reserves

Assets denominated in foreign currencies held by a country's monetary authorities (in the United States, held by the Federal Reserve System and the Treasury Department).

open market

Freely competitive market.

open market operations

Purchases and sales of securities, typically U.S. Treasury securities, in the open market, by the Open Market Trading Desk at the Federal Reserve Bank of New York as directed by the Federal Open Market Committee, to influence interest rates. Purchases increase the supply of Federal Reserve balances to depository institutions; sales do the opposite.

outright transaction

"Permanent" purchase or sale of securities in the open market, or the redemption of securities, by the Federal Reserve to adjust the supply of balances at the Federal Reserve Banks over the long term. (Contrasts with transactions intended to adjust the supply of balances only temporarily. *See* **repurchase agreement** *and* **reverse repurchase agreement**.)

over the counter

Figurative term for the means of trading securities that are not listed on an organized stock exchange such as the New York Stock Exchange. Over-the-counter trading is done by broker-dealers who communicate by telephone and computer networks.

P

paper

General term for short-term debt instruments such as commercial paper.

payments system

Collective term for mechanisms (both paper-based and electronic) for moving funds, payments, and money among financial institutions throughout the nation. The Federal Reserve plays a major role in the nation's payments system through distribution of currency and coin, processing of checks, and electronic transfer of funds; various private organizations also perform payments system functions.

portfolio
Collection of loans or assets, classified by type of borrower or asset. For example, a bank's portfolio might include loans, investment securities, and assets managed in trust; the loan portfolio might include commercial, mortgage, and consumer installment loans.

presentment fee
Fee that a bank receiving a check imposes on the bank collecting payment.

prompt corrective action
Supervisory framework, created under the Federal Deposit Insurance Corporation Improvement Act of 1991, that links enforcement actions closely to the level of capital held by banks.

R

real interest rates
Interest rates adjusted for the expected erosion of purchasing power resulting from inflation. Technically defined as nominal interest rates minus the expected rate of inflation. (*Compare* **nominal interest rates**.)

reciprocal currency (swap) arrangements
Short-term reciprocal arrangements between a Federal Reserve Bank and individual foreign central banks. By drawing on a swap the foreign central bank obtains dollars that can be used to conduct foreign exchange intervention in support of its currency or to lend to its domestic banking system to satisfy temporary liquidity demands. For the duration of the swap, the Federal Reserve Bank obtains an equivalent amount of foreign currency along with a commitment from the foreign central bank to repurchase the foreign currency at a preset exchange rate.

Reports of Condition and Income
Quarterly financial report that all banks, savings and loan associations, Edge and agreement corporations, and certain other types of organizations must file with a federal regulatory agency. Informally called a Call Report.

repurchase agreement (RP or repo)
A transaction in which the Federal Reserve enters into an agreement with a primary dealer to acquire securities from the dealer for a specified

principal amount at an agreed-upon interest rate and to return the securities on a specified future date. The maturity date may be the next day or many days later, with the maximum length set by the FOMC. These transactions permit the Federal Reserve to increase the supply of Federal Reserve balances for the length of the agreement.

required reserve balance

That portion of its required reserves that a depository institution must hold in an account at a Federal Reserve Bank. This portion is the difference between the institution's reserve requirement and its vault cash.

required reserve ratio

The percentage of reservable liabilities that depository institutions must set aside in the form of reserves.

required reserves

Funds that a depository institution is required to maintain in the form of vault cash or, if vault cash is insufficient to meet the requirement, in the form of a balance maintained directly with a Reserve Bank or indirectly with a pass-through correspondent bank. The required amount varies according to the required reserve ratios set by the Board and the amount of reservable liabilities held by the institution.

reservable liabilities

Those obligations on a depository institution's balance sheet that are subject to reserve requirements. Transaction deposits, nonpersonal time deposits, and Eurocurrency liabilities are all subject to reserve requirements; however, the required reserve ratios for nonpersonal time deposits and Eurocurrency liabilities are zero.

reserve requirements

Requirements set by the Board of Governors for the amounts of certain liabilities that depository institutions must set aside in the form of reserves.

reverse repurchase agreement

A transaction—the opposite of a repurchase agreement—in which the Federal Reserve enters into an agreement with a primary dealer to sell securities from the System portfolio for a specified principal amount at an agreed-upon interest rate and to receive the securities back from the dealer on a specified future date. The maturity date may be the next day or many days later, with the maximum length set by the FOMC. These transactions permit the Federal Reserve to decrease the supply of Federal Reserve balances for the length of the agreement.

S

savings and loan association (S&L)

Historically, depository institution that accepted deposits mainly from individuals and invested heavily in residential mortgage loans; although still primarily residential lenders, S&Ls now have many of the powers of commercial banks.

savings bank

Depository institution historically engaged primarily in accepting consumer savings deposits and in originating and investing in residential mortgage loans; now may offer checking-type deposits and make a wider range of loans. (*Compare* **commercial bank**.)

savings bond

A nonmarketable debt obligation of the U.S. government. Savings bonds are available in both paper and book-entry form and can be purchased with an initial investment of as little as $25. Investors can purchase paper savings bonds in person from many depository institutions, by mail from a Reserve Bank or the Treasury, or online. Book-entry bonds are available from the Treasury online.

securities

Paper certificates (definitive securities) or electronic records (book-entry securities) evidencing ownership of equity (stocks) or debt obligations (bonds).

securitization

The process of packaging and selling similar financial instruments, such as loans and other receivables, in the form of "asset-backed" securities that can be traded on secondary markets. Securitization allows financial institutions to transfer some of the risks of ownership to parties more willing or able to manage them.

self-regulatory organizations

Associations of broker-dealers or others that have responsibility, under the oversight of the Securities and Exchange Commission, to regulate their own members through the adoption and enforcement of rules of conduct for fair, ethical, and efficient practices. Examples include the National Association of Securities Dealers and the New York Stock Exchange.

settlement

In banking, the process of recording the debit and credit positions of two parties in a transfer of funds. Also, the delivery of securities by a seller and the payment by the buyer.

shock

Unanticipated or unusual event that has a noticeable impact on the economy or a financial system.

special drawing rights (SDRs)

Type of international reserve asset created by the International Monetary Fund and allocated, on occasion, to the nations that are members of the IMF.

state bank

Bank that is chartered by a state; may or may not be a member of the Federal Reserve System.

subsidiary

Company that is controlled by another corporation (called the parent corporation), typically through stock ownership or voting control.

substitute check

A paper reproduction of an original check that contains an image of the front and back of the original check and is suitable for automated processing, just as the original check is. The Check Clearing for the 21st Century Act, commonly known as Check 21, allows depository institutions to truncate original checks, process check information electronically, and deliver substitute checks to depository institutions if they require paper checks.

swap

An agreement between two parties to exchange cash flows of underlying securities. For example, in an interest rate swap, the most common type of swap, one party agrees to pay a fixed interest rate in return for receiving a variable rate from the other party.

swap arrangement

See **reciprocal currency arrangement**.

System Open Market Account

The Federal Reserve's portfolio of U.S. Treasury securities. Purchases and sales in this account—open market operations—are under the overall supervision of the manager of the System Open Market Account, subject to the policies and rules of the Federal Open Market Committee.

systemic risk

Risk that a disruption at a firm, in a market segment, to a settlement system, or in a similar setting will cause widespread difficulties at other firms, in other market segments, or in the financial system as a whole.

T

thrift institution

A general term encompassing savings banks, savings and loan associations, and credit unions.

Thrift Institutions Advisory Council

Group established by the Board of Governors to obtain information and opinions on the needs and problems of thrift institutions. Made up of representatives of savings and loan associations, savings banks, and credit unions.

tightening

Federal Reserve action to raise interest rates. Undertaken when inflation is a concern. (*Compare* **easing**.)

time deposit

Funds deposited in an account that has a fixed term to maturity and technically cannot be withdrawn before maturity without advance notice (for example, a certificate of deposit). Time deposits may earn interest.

Trading Desk (the Desk)

The group at the Federal Reserve Bank of New York that conducts open market operations for the Federal Reserve System and intervenes in foreign currency markets for the Federal Reserve and Treasury.

transaction account

A checking account or similar deposit account from which transfers of funds can be made. Demand deposit accounts, NOW (negotiable order of withdrawal) accounts, and credit union share draft accounts are examples of transaction accounts.

U

U.S. Treasury securities

Obligations of the U.S. government issued by the U.S. Department of the Treasury as a means of borrowing money to meet government expenditures not covered by tax revenues. All marketable Treasury securities have a minimum purchase amount of $1,000 and are issued in $1,000 increments. There are three types of marketable Treasury securities: bills, notes, and bonds.

- **Treasury bill (T-bill)**
  Short-term U.S. Treasury security having a maturity of up to one year. T-bills are sold at a discount. Investors purchase a bill at a price lower than the face value (for example, the investor might buy a

$10,000 bill for $9,700); the return is the difference between the price paid and the amount received when the bill is sold or it matures (if held to maturity, the return on the T-bill in the example would be $300).

- **Treasury note**
  Intermediate-term security having a maturity of one to ten years. Notes pay interest semiannually, and the principal is payable at maturity.

- **Treasury bond**
  Long-term security having a maturity of longer than ten years. Bonds pay interest semiannually, and the principal is payable at maturity.

The Treasury Department also issues several types of nonmarketable securities, including savings bonds.

V

vault cash
Cash on hand at a depository institution to meet day-to-day business needs, such as cashing checks for customers. Can be used to satisfy the institution's reserve requirement.

W

wire transfer
Electronic transfer of funds; usually involves large-dollar payments.

Index